EXPANDING ELEMENTARY TEACHER EDUCATION THROUGH SERVICE-LEARNING

EXPANDING ELEMENTARY TEACHER EDUCATION THROUGH SERVICE-LEARNING

A Handbook on Extending Literacy Field Experience for Twenty-First-Century Urban Teacher Preparation

Margaret-Mary Sulentic Dowell and Tynisha D. Meidl

ROWMAN & LITTLEFIELD
Lanham • Boulder • New York • London

Published by Rowman & Littlefield
A wholly owned subsidiary of The Rowman & Littlefield Publishing Group,
Inc.
4501 Forbes Boulevard, Suite 200, Lanham, Maryland 20706
www.rowman.com

Unit A, Whitacre Mews, 26-34 Stannary Street, London SE11 4AB

British Library Cataloguing in Publication Information Available

Library of Congress Cataloging-in-Publication Data

Names: Dowell, Margaret-Mary Sulentic, 1957- author. | Meidl, Tynisha D., 1980- author.
Title: Expanding elementary teacher education through service-learning : a handbook on extend-
    ing literacy field experience for twenty-first-century urban teacher preparation / Margaret-
    Mary Sulentic Dowell and Tynisha D. Meidl.
Description: Lanham : Rowman & Littlefield, [2017] | Includes bibliographical references.
Identifiers: LCCN 2016031046 (print) | LCCN 2016040900 (ebook) | ISBN 9781475825879
    (cloth : alk. paper) | ISBN 9781475825886 (pbk. : alk. paper) | ISBN 9781475825893 (Elec-
    tronic)
Subjects: LCSH: Elementary school teachers--Training of--United States--Handbooks, manuals,
    etc. | Education, Urban--Fieldwork--United States--Handbooks, manuals, etc. | Language arts
    (Elementary)--United States--Handbooks, manuals, etc. | Service learning--United States--
    Handbooks, manuals, etc.
Classification: LCC LB1715 .D65 2017 (print) | LCC LB1715 (ebook) | DDC 370.71/1--dc23
LC record available at https://lccn.loc.gov/2016031046

Printed in the United States of America

CONTENTS

PREFACE

The goal of this handbook is to offer teacher educators a blueprint for how they can strengthen and extend traditional literacy field experiences to include service-learning components, expanding teacher education to better prepare elementary education candidates to meet the needs of children in twenty-first-century urban elementary classrooms. We wrote this text considering the need to redefine teacher education in regard to literacy. For the past decade in the United States, the teaching profession has faced increased scrutiny, and teaching has been framed and blamed for many social ills.

The teaching profession has been ridiculed, scorned, and mocked. Teacher education has been put under a microscope and, in many instances, rightly so as little reform in how we prepare teachers has occurred. Teacher education programs and colleges of education face a complex and multifaceted task of preparing teachers to teach in an increasingly bifurcated system where children of color comprise a significant number of urban school populations, yet the teaching force remains predominantly White, female, monolingual, and middle income (American Educational Research Association, 1991; Ayres & Ford, 1996; Compton-Lilly, 2004; Delpit, 1995; Freedman, Simons, Kalnin, & Casareno, 1999). In addition, the racial and the socioeconomic makeup of many faculty mirrors the incoming teacher candidate population.

As literacy teacher educators, our intent is to demonstrate how teacher education can be transformed to include more authentic and meaningful field experience by incorporating service-learning components into medial field experience opportunities and placements, more adequately preparing teachers to teach literacy in urban elementary classrooms.

According to a study commissioned by the American Association of Colleges for Teacher Education, approximately 1,300 traditional teacher preparation programs exist in the United States (Koppich & Merseth, 2000); alternative preparation programs are increasing. The preparation of teachers is complex, situated in local communities and institutions where local policy and politics impact preparation (American Educational Research Association, 1991). This dynamic creates tensions and a dissonance between the lived experiences of teachers, which can be markedly different than the lived experiences of the students whom they teach (Barnes, 2006; Cochran-Smith, 2000; Delpit, 1995).

As authors of the American Educational Research Association's special panel report claimed, "Teacher turnover is the largest single determinant of demand for new teachers." The annual turnover rate hovers at approximately 30 percent (1991, p. 6). Perhaps lack of adequate preparation, particularly in the experiences that lead to effective teaching, correlates to high turnover rates.

Outcomes for this proposed handbook include a deeper understanding of how intersection of the "traditional" field experience and service-learning prepares pre-service teachers to teach literacy. Course-embedded service-learning components strengthen literacy field experiences so that pre-service teachers expand their frames of reference and begin to grasp community needs and deepen civic responsibility. Several cases serve as models of how to cultivate community-university partnerships and craft literacy field experience placements that include service-learning components focused on literacy learning and teaching.

Another goal of this manual is increasing expertise in how to assess school literacy needs when seeking out partners and placements, matching those to the needs of pre-service teachers. Finally, methods of how to build collaboration and generate commitment, as well as strategies for how to organize, manage, and evaluate service-learning field experiences are included for individual literacy faculty, literacy program faculty, and entire teacher education programs.

ACKNOWLEDGMENTS

MARGARET-MARY'S ACKNOWLEDGMENTS

A heartfelt thank you goes first to my husband, Tony, for his patience and understanding as I embarked upon this book venture. You supported me 100 percent, even when I was most difficult, and you believed in my abilities when I faltered. I love you for many reasons but especially for keeping me grounded.

I also wish to thank my students for the lessons they have taught me; I may have been the person in charge—the professor of record—but from you I learned the true value of observing and listening and what a community of learners entails. Through you I was reminded of the dissonance that exists in the tenuous space between just being a teacher education candidate and becoming a pre-service teacher—that excitement as you assume your teacher identities.

A special thanks goes to my colleagues in the School of Education at Louisiana State University (LSU)—Renée Casbergue, my forever mentor; Cyn DiCarlo, the best cheerleader a person could have; and Sassy Wheeler, for your cool confidence and panache. Thank you Marybeth Lima for your visionary service-learning leadership at LSU and the space you provided to conceive this book. Thanks also to the teachers and educators in the East Baton Rouge Parish School System—Catasha Edwards, Heather Carpenter, Rachel Stallworth, Mary Hotard, and Bonnie Wilder—you are my partners in preparation.

Thank you Ty, for being a friend, colleague, and confidant. You made this journey enjoyable!

And finally, thank you to Sarah Jubar, acquisitions editor at Rowman & Littlefield.

TYNISHA'S ACKNOWLEDGEMENTS

To my daughters, Neenah and Nevaeh, thank you for being such a blessing in this year of transition. I appreciate the days you played outside so that I could write. To my spouse, Christopher, thank you for all of your words of encouragement and random text messages reminding me to write.

Thank you to my family, friends, and colleagues. I appreciate the unique ways you have invested in my success as an individual and scholar—thank you. A special thank you is in order for St. Norbert College, teacher education students, and the Sturzl Center for Community Engagement. To be a teacher is truly to touch a life forever, and you have shown me that in countless ways. I appreciate St. Norbert College for being an institution that creates an environment for me to live out the mission of the college through my teaching and scholarship.

Margaret-Mary, thank you for being a fantastic mentor, colleague, and friend. Thank you for introducing me to service-learning and helping me contribute to this field of study.

Most importantly, I give honor to God for sustaining me through this project and for continually blessing me.

INTRODUCTION

The purpose of this handbook is to serve as a resource guide for teacher educators to more adequately prepare elementary teacher education candidates to teach literacy successfully in urban schools or nontraditional urban settings and sites. As society shifts so should the methods used regarding how best to prepare teachers to successfully teach at the elementary grades (1–5) in urban contexts.

After briefly describing the three levels of field experience and service-learning, the handbook draws upon the authors' expertise and offers vignettes and case studies that have successfully incorporated service-learning into medial literacy field experiences. Subsequent chapters highlight how to cultivate community-university partnerships and establish literacy field experience placements, how to craft collaboration and generate commitment, as well as how to organize, manage, and evaluate literacy service-learning field experiences.

The bulk of the handbook targets teacher education faculty within teacher preparation programs, but the handbook can also be used to assist teachers, teacher leaders, and district personnel. This includes faculty teaching literacy methods courses, directors of field experience, and administrators who supervise these programs as well as district personal that serve as liaisons between university program faculty and districts and schools as a secondary audience.

I

FIELD EXPERIENCE AND SERVICE-LEARNING: PREPARING ELEMENTARY TEACHERS FOR TWENTY-FIRST-CENTURY URBAN TEACHING

Teaching is difficult, demanding, and draining work. Teaching is difficult in that it requires differentiated skills, orchestration, flexibility, and stamina. Teaching is demanding as teachers cannot uniformly apply a formula for instruction or unvaryingly employ a script that ensures meeting students where they enter a class and extending knowledge and skill forward over time. Rather, teachers assess individual strengths and weaknesses and plan instruction accordingly—with individuals, in small groups, and in whole group configurations while feeding curiosity, innovation, and creativity.

Teaching is draining work, both physically and mentally. It is complex and messy; part art, part science, it is much more than just telling others what you know (or think you know). Teaching requires more than just subject knowledge, no matter the depth of that knowledge—it necessitates pedagogical skill, content knowledge, organization, collaboration, and well-developed communication skills. Teaching also calls for an acute knowledge, understanding, and acceptance of the children in any given classroom, in any particular school and school district, and the communities from which children hail.

TWENTY-FIRST-CENTURY CHALLENGES TO TEACHER EDUCATION

For the past decade in the United States, the teaching profession has faced increasing scrutiny. Unfairly, teaching has been framed and blamed for many social ills. Teachers have been ridiculed, scorned, and mocked. The teaching profession has been commoditized, assaulted by business and corporate interests seeking to develop a market share. Is the education profession guilty of being mired in the past, as some claim? Yes. After all, education still uses an agrarian (nine-month) calendar, yet a majority of the 59 million children enrolled in Pre-K through twelfth grade in the United States simply do not need the summer off to pick crops.

In 2011, the US Census Bureau, utilizing the American Community Survey (ACS) and the Current Population Survey (CPS), two sources of school enrollment data, reported the following:

- 5 million children in Pre-K programs,
- 4 million children in kindergarten,
- 33 million students enrolled in first through eighth grades, and
- 17 million in ninth through twelfth grades.

This equates to a staggering number of children who need and deserve the highest quality education.

With such high stakes (no pun intended) the training of teachers becomes a paramount concern as a means of furthering a democratic society, as an economic driver, and as the US constitution ensures, an equalizer and means of achieving "life, liberty, and the pursuit of happiness."

Education programs need stellar candidates and the resources to craft programs that produce high-quality educators. Do all programs need to have a cookie-cutter approach and uniform courses and course sequence? No. Those who chose teaching as a profession, those teachers who consciously decided they were going to be great at their craft and who work at being better every day, know that teacher preparation demands excellent training and carefully sequenced, intentional experiences to build both pedagogy and content (Darling-Hammond, 2014a).

Teacher preparation faculty need to work in tandem with school-based personnel, "faculty in the field," as partners in preparation. Teachers are made—they are not born. Darling-Hammond (2006a) confronts this myth asserting that teacher education programs need "systematic, sustained initiatives to ensure that all teachers have the opportunity to become well prepared" (Darling-Hammond, 2006b, p. ix).

WHO WE ARE

As teacher educators who share a passion for teacher education, teaching, and learning, but who followed different paths to our current careers, we believe that the essential core of preparation—the basic, fundamental crux of preparing quality teachers—lies in shaping programs that provide optimum learning experience in classrooms and communities yet remain flexible and responsive to the shifting demands and needs of society.

Margaret-Mary completed her field experiences within a traditional teacher education program in a formal "normal school" in the Midwest. Her placements ranged from a University Laboratory School to urban schools in northeast Iowa. She earned her BA in 1979, has been teaching for thirty-six years, and she was one of the first in the nation to achieve National Board Certified Teacher status, recertifying for the third time in 2015.

Tynisha's (Ty) alternative route to teacher education was different from Margaret-Mary's traditional preparation pathway in that she became a first generation Teach for America (TFA) corps member in 2002. She taught in both the Baltimore City Public Schools and in the Rio Grande Valley in Texas. She has been an educator for thirteen years.

Both Margaret-Mary and Ty came to service-learning by varied pathways as well. Early in her first teacher educator position, Margaret-Mary was a service-learning faculty fellow at the University of Southern Mississippi in Hattiesburg. Her journey began there but she has consistently employed service-learning since 2001, honing her knowledge and experience and including intentional service-learning components embedded into field experiences for elementary educators involved in their professional practice coursework.

When she encountered service-learning, Ty was seeking a better way to prepare her teacher education candidates who attend a Catholic liberal arts institution. She crafted a unique intersession experience in 2007, bringing her students to New Orleans each year since for an intensive weeklong field experience in order to provide them with strategic urban teaching experience post–Hurricane Katrina.

Ty and Margaret-Mary met when Ty contacted Margaret-Mary about a 2007 service-learning publication. Via e-mail, Ty explained that she was interested in creating an intensive medial service-learning opportunity for her students over winter break wherein her students would assist with a community charter school's students who had literacy needs. When an anticipated trip to New Orleans materialized, Ty traveled from her home in the Midwest to Margaret-Mary's home, where they met and forged a collegial friendship.

Both Margaret-Mary and Ty sought out service-learning as a more meaningful way to prepare teacher education students. Both employ service-learning within literacy coursework consistently within their respective teacher education programs. Although their teacher education experiences vary in terms of geographical locations, years in the field, and preparation pathways, they believe that enriching and strengthening field experience through embedded service-learning components is the answer to how to best prepare teachers to teach optimally in twenty-first-century urban elementary classrooms.

DEFINING FIELD EXPERIENCE

Within teacher preparation programs, future teachers need to participate as early as possible and as frequently as possible with children, classrooms, schools, teachers, and communities in order to be prepared for the needs and challenges of their future students. This apprenticeship model means that pre-service teachers are placed with master teachers. Yet, this is a seemingly simplistic solution to a multifaceted issue.

In essence, twenty-first-century teacher preparation programs and teacher educators face a conundrum—these preparation programs are attempting to prepare teacher education candidates for an unknown future. Issues that impact teacher preparation such as evolving technology, increasingly sophisticated information processing, safe school environments, and the influence of rapid societal changes all contribute to the task of preparing teachers.

Historically, student teaching has been viewed as a capstone clinical experience and perhaps privileged as being a more important preparation experience. However, the significance of field experience components in teacher preparation programming has emerged as paramount as typical education candidates transition from student to beginning teacher (Appelt Slick, 1995; Darling-Hammond, 2006a, 2010a, 2010b, and 2014).

GOALS OF FIELD EXPERIENCE: VIEWING CLASSROOMS AS CLINICS

Field experience, described as early teacher preparation experience, may be referred to in many ways including the terms practicum or clinical experience. Jaquith describes field experience as "early contact hours with children or clinical experiences, some sort of practicum or mid-tier field experiences often associated with methods courses" (1995, p. 13).

Typically, three levels describe the range of field experiences found in most teacher education programs. The first level—initial field experience—is frequently incorporated into beginning professional practice coursework and usually includes structured observations designed to provide pre-service teachers with a realistic view of the workings of a classroom as a microcosm of a school.

These observations should be designed so that pre-service teachers have objectives within observations such as mapping a room's arrangement, observing and cataloging the print-rich literacy environment of a room, or possibly observing teacher-student interactions during instruction and transitions.

Included as well in initial field experiences are opportunities to engage in low-level teacher activities such as assisting a host teacher with displaying student work, preparing instructional materials, administering makeup quizzes, or possibly grading student work. The more pre-service teachers are actively and authentically involved and the higher the degree of collaboration between host teacher, university faculty, or preparation provider, the more sophisticated the field experience for pre-service teachers. And, the higher the level of involvement and the deeper the collaboration, the more realistic the pre-service teacher's views are about teaching.

The second level of field experience, often called medial field experiences, are depicted as opportunities to experience more varied and increasingly more involved tasks concomitant with teaching. An increase of teacher-oriented activities is typically associated with methods courses. Examples include one-to-one tutoring, small group instruction, whole group instruction, conducting assessment activities, instructional design (lesson planning), and gradually assuming more direct responsibility for students, for longer periods of time or specific to a content area connected to a course.

Third level or final field experiences operate as an apprenticeship or internship. These third level experiences are referred to as either student teaching or as a teaching internship. Final field experiences are characterized by experiences that transfer the locus of authority from cooperating teacher of record to student teacher in an increasingly scaffolded manner. Tharpe (2014) and Coffman and Patterson (2014) call for this experience to resemble the medical model of a residency.

All of these experiences are important; however, the merit of initial and medial field experiences determines the quality of the final field experience which directly impacts the preparedness of the pre-service teacher to assume his or her own classroom as a highly qualified novice teacher. Darling-Hammond calls for seven features that are needed to prepare teachers for twenty-first-century classrooms:

1. A common, clear vision of good teaching that permeates all coursework and clinical experiences, creating a coherent set of learning experiences
2. Well-defined standards of professional practice and performance that are used to guide and evaluate coursework and clinical work
3. A strong core curriculum taught in the context of practice and grounded in knowledge of child and adolescent development and learning, an understanding of social and cultural contexts, curriculum, assessment, and subject matter pedagogy

4. Extended clinical experiences—at least 30 weeks of supervised practicum and student teaching opportunities in each program— that are carefully chosen to support the ideas presented in simultaneous, closely interwoven coursework

5. Extensive use of case methods, teacher research, performance assessments, and portfolio evaluation that apply learning to real problems of practice

6. Explicit strategies to help students to confront their own deep-seated beliefs and assumptions about learning and students and to learn about the experiences of people different from themselves

7. Strong relationships, common knowledge, and shared beliefs among school- and university-based faculty jointly engaged in transforming teaching, schooling, and teacher education (Darling-Hammond, 2006a, p. 6).

With a focus on the efficacy of Darling-Hammond's recommendation that supervised clinical practicum, or what are referred to as field experiences, are carefully and intentionally selected to reinforce and validate course concepts and course ideas as well as aligned with course goals, the embodiment of service-learning is embedding course goals and service-learning in an interconnected and interwoven manner. In particular, features 4, 6, and 7 listed above can be achieved through embedded service-learning experiences in carefully crafted field work. It is those medial practicum field experiences that provide the focus for this handbook.

DEFINING SERVICE-LEARNING

Service-learning is a form of experiential education that allows students to learn by doing with roots in the progressive educational movement work of John Dewey (1922; 1938). While many definitions of service-learning exist, we employ Furco's (2000) description of service-learning as a teaching method that incorporates some aspect of community need and involvement embedded into existing coursework in a mutually beneficial, reciprocal relationship.

Course-related community involvement enhances students' under-standing of course materials while deepening the learning process; in addition, in service-learning courses, students build a sense of civic responsibility as they address community-identified needs through course goals, objectives, and strategic experiences.

In service-learning courses, the community serves as kind of a "lived text" for the class—affording a significant and influential source of in-formation to complement robust course content—readings, demonstra-tions, activities, and discussions. Service-learning is a powerful peda-gogical tool that provides a meaningful linkage for students.

Tai-Seale explains that within service-learning courses, objectives are aligned to the collective needs of a community partner in order to achieve mutual benefits for the partner as well as students enrolled in the university course (2001). Butin (2003) notes that in service-learning, course learning goals and objectives are internalized through carefully selected and sequentially structured experiences, connecting course-embedded service with academic learning.

Reflection is an integral part of service-learning, used as a means of promoting deep thought and consideration of the experience that re-sults in personal growth and heightened civic responsibility (Eyler, Giles, & Schmiede, 1996). Reflection is an equally important tool used within teacher education (Canning, 1991) as pre-service teachers think deeply and consider the experience they are acquiring as they gain knowledge, skill, and proficiency in teaching and expertise.

EXTENDING FIELD EXPERIENCE THROUGH SERVICE-LEARNING: TEACHER PREPARATION FOR THE TWENTY-FIRST-CENTURY

Maxwell (2014) reports that in the 2014–2015 academic year, African American, Asian, Latino, and Native American public school students together outnumber non-Hispanic Whites in K–12 public schools (National Center for Educational Statistics, 2014). In a recent report of survey results of the US public teaching force, Feistritzer states the number of K–12 teachers who are White is 84 percent (2011, p. 15). This difference between students and their teachers creates a disso-nance of experience.

To develop sensitivity among pre-service teachers and increase sensitivity among in-service teachers while honing the skills necessary to teach from a culturally responsive perspective, teacher educators should recognize, confront, and address the tensions that result when teachers differ from the public school student populations they teach. Teacher educators should explicitly address the educational impact of economic, ethnic, and various cultural differences (Delpit, 1995; Freedman, Simons, Kalnin, & Casareno, 1999).

Intentionality from colleges and universities is needed to reduce this tension as well as provide authentic experiences for teacher candidates at all levels. A specific way to address the dissonance that may arise due to economic, cultural, racial, ethnic, and linguistic diversity is by incorporating and imbedding community-based service-learning components.

Over two decades ago, Appelt Slick urged that, "teacher education students need placements with outstanding teachers who can serve as role models" (1995, p. 150). While the demands and challenges of teaching have amplified and the rigor involved in teaching has increased, the prominence of quality medial field experiences as a shaping force in teacher preparation continues to necessitate outstanding host teachers who can function as role models and mentors.

Medial field experience has emerged as a crucial factor and a key preparation feature. The stronger the medial field experience, the better prepared a pre-service teacher is to engage in student teaching and the more qualified he or she is to subsequently teach.

Intentional, well-planned, strategic, and carefully crafted medial field experiences are the backbone of a teacher education program. These medial experiences can be greatly enhanced by including service-learning components consistent with course goals and embedded into methods courses. Based on our experiences in teacher education, in order to prepare teachers for twenty-first-century classrooms, the following six concerns should be considered when planning medial service-learning field experiences:

1. Include reflective practice at strategic intervals throughout field experiences;
2. Seek increasingly diverse public school classrooms or context in terms of religious background, economics, ethnicity, race, gen-

der, language, sexual orientation/gender expression, and special needs;

3. Consider legal issues with field experience;
4. Provide access to technological and information innovations, including new literacies;
5. Remain cognizant of developing teacher leaders; and
6. Be mindful of the need for pre-service teachers' induction and/or orientation experiences.

In traditional teacher education programs, field experiences are often supplemental to coursework occurring within a program of study, with the field experiences frequently performed as an *addendum* to students' coursework. In our experience, field experiences have often appeared as an afterthought, a lab component treated as a compliance issue versus a rich learning experience. When service-learning is incorporated into teacher education field experiences, the service is integrated *within* the course, an important distinction.

To cultivate thoughtfulness toward urban teaching, coherent and relevant culturally responsive theories, resultant pedagogy, and strategic field experiences throughout the entire teacher preparation sequence deepen teacher education candidates' awareness, respect, and acceptance of urban contexts (Darling-Hammond, 2006a). In particular, the medial experiences become shaping experiences, allowing pre-service teachers to absorb initial experiences as practices to emulate and implement during the medial phase. Strong medial experiences equate to better preparation to teach students, and thus better overall preparation.

By delivering focused, strategic, and intentional service-learning field experience activities situated in urban schools and communities, teacher education programming can be significantly improved, more appropriately and adequately preparing students to teach successfully in urban environments.

The preparation of teachers is complex work, "situated in local communities and institutions where local policy and politics impact preparation" (American Educational Research Association, 1991, p. 3). This dynamic creates tensions and a dissonance between the lived experiences of teachers which can be markedly different than the lived experiences of the students whom they teach (Barnes, 2006; Cochran-Smith, 2000; Delpit, 1995).

This dissonance between students' and teachers' respective backgrounds and lived experiences equates to more complex, more demanding, and intricate instruction in teacher education programming to prepare teachers for these increasing responsibilities. According to Boyle-Baise, courses with service-learning components can positively influence pre-service teachers' dispositions, typically resulting in improved classroom practice (2002).

According to several leading scholars in the field of teacher education in urban environs, a carefully crafted, strategic, and sequential set of field experiences safeguards that pre-service teachers enter the workforce as culturally responsive teachers (Barnes, 2006; Cochran-Smith, 2000; Gay, 2000; Irvine, 2003; Larkin & Sleeter, 1995; Mason & Schumm, 2003; Villegas & Lucas, 2002).

Service-learning field experiences address both the tensions created by the differences in background between many urban students and the teachers who teach them by engaging university pre-service teachers in course-embedded, structured opportunities that scaffold experiences which, in turn, broaden their cultural spheres and widen their perspectives (Boyle-Baise & Sleeter, 2000).

In this chapter we presented challenges that face teacher education, especially challenges of teaching children who will inhabit the majority of their lives in a twenty-first-century world. Within the context of teacher education, the authors shared their journey as literacy scholars and service-learning practitioners. In addition, a working definition of both field experience and service-learning was offered. Finally, the authors shared medial literacy service-learning as a pedagogical pathway, a means of extending field experience in meaningful ways. While teaching at any level is important, the focus of this handbook is on the elementary grades 1–5. In chapter 2, we will provide background that assists readers with understanding the unique context of urban education.

2

THE EFFICACY OF SERVICE-LEARNING EMBEDDED FIELD EXPERIENCES IN URBAN TEACHER PREPARATION

Urban education presents a distinctive context in the United States. Urban teaching and learning implies that the process of education itself provides access and equity to children as a social justice issue. According to Darling-Hammond, a simplified definition of urban education connotes areas of dense, diverse populations in terms of representing multiethnic, multiracial, and multilinguistic geographical areas that are also marked by poverty (2014b). An awareness of the distinct issues that exist in many urban areas in the United States is crucial to understanding the unique challenges urban environs—schools, districts, and communities—offer teacher education.

UNDERSTANDING THE URBAN CONTEXT

While it is easy to typify and perhaps oversimplify the urban environ of education in the United States, understanding the context of urban teaching is crucial. As a more current description, urban teaching signifies under-resourced schools (not underperforming) that struggle to meet the intensifying needs of children who lack critical basic supports including adequate housing, access to primary healthcare, and what Darling-Hammond (2014b) refers to as food security. An under-resourced school could lack an adequate library, or employ an overabundance of novice teachers, or fail to provide necessary services children require such as bilingual or speech teachers.

This landscape paints a portrait of schools populated with children who hail from families and communities that are characterized by a lack of access to opportunity, specifically health and human services resources; children who live in extreme pockets of poverty; children of color; children of immigrants as well as immigrant children and, thus, many second language learners; children who are segregated by income level, race, ethnicity, and often language and linguistic uniqueness, and underfunded schools. This depiction calls for supports that address such inequities but also for teacher preparation that acknowledges and addresses the intense challenges of urban education.

Research and best practices related to teaching and learning within this context are not a recent development. The United States has a history of poor, immigrant populations with extreme needs inhabiting urban areas. Turn-of-the-century police reporter turned social reformer and photographer, Jacob Riis, documented the living conditions of New York City (NYC) tenements beginning in 1890 in the seminal photographic work, *How the Other Half Lives* (Madison & Riis, 1971).

At the time of publication, NYC's population was an estimated million-and-a-half, and one-third of the population lived in poverty, isolated by income as well as by ethnicity, with scarce access to food (Madison & Riis, 1971, p. 191). Riis was one of a few to photograph, capture, and preserve living conditions in the slums of NYC where it was estimated that as many as 300,000 people per square mile were crowded into tenements on the Lower East Side. Riis documented what life was like, how such slums came into existence, and who resided in these tenements, establishing an historical record of what US urban living looked like for many.

Similarly, Coan (1977) authenticated immigrant life, accessing the Ellis Island Oral History Project's collection of interviews as a primary source to document the 12 million who came to the United States between 1892 and 1954. Preceding the Irish wave of immigration of 1845–1849, Coan selected 114 cases that illustrated again a tradition of poverty, crowded conditions, ethnic segregation, and stressful living conditions. One would think such conditions would be ameliorated over time and urban centers would receive the resources needed and deserved.

In 2003, the then International Reading Association (IRA) (since renamed the International Literacy Association) highlighted the conditions in urban US cities issuing a policy update entitled, *Addressing Urban Education Needs*. This policy update was a result of a partnership between IRA, the National Urban Alliance for Effective Education, and the Urban Partnership for Literacy, and the City Heights Project of San Diego, California, examining urban education and drawing attention to the issue.

In tandem, Kozol (2006) compared segregated urban centers in the United States to the apartheid system of South Africa, an alarming comparison. Like Kozol, the authors of this book acknowledge the result of concentrations of poverty and want to point out that a hungry child, or a child that lacks basic health services and may suffer from frequent sickness, cannot learn in the same manner and at the same pace as a child who does not encounter such challenges. While poverty cannot be blamed for some of the unique challenges faced by urban education, it is a collective responsibility to address how poverty plays out in educational arenas.

The IRA policy update delineated the boundaries of urban education, positing that 50 percent of children in the United States live in cities, many of them in poverty, and presented what the IRA termed a "compelling profile of needs" regarding how educators can best meet the educational needs of urban children. In addition, the policy update highlighted historical issues between urban children and a lack of access to healthcare, overrepresentation of children of color identified for special education services, culture and language dissonance, and a lack of access to quality literacy and libraries (International Reading Association, May 2003).

The policy update echoes Milner and Lomotey's assertion that urban areas are dense, large metroplexes distinguished by a breadth of student diversity, including racial, ethnic, religious, language, and socioeconomic differences (2014). Further, both Milner and Lomotey and the IRA policy update similarly portray urban education as stymied by high poverty coupled with a lack of culturally responsive teaching, weak pedagogy, and inadequate funding in addition to a paucity of access to opportunity.

Despite the differing waves of immigration that have impacted urban centers—such as the Irish immigrants who came to the United

States from 1845–1849 following the infamous potato famine; an influx of Chinese in the 1800s; the significant number of White, northern Europeans who immigrated from Germany, Ireland, Austria, Hungary, England, Scotland, Wales, Russia, and Sweden as well as from Southern Italy from 1820 through 1931, including the large numbers who immigrated post–World War II who identified as Jewish, German, Japanese, or Italian—immigrants tend to settle in enclaves (Coan, 1977, pp. xxv–xxix).

In a similar fashion the Southeast Asian immigrants, notably the Vietnamese in the late 1970s, also followed this pattern of settling in ethnic neighborhoods. The border states experience the same patterns of settlement with Caribbean, Mexican, and Central American immigrants clustering in ethnic urban neighborhoods in large urban centers such as Miami, New Orleans, Houston, Phoenix, and Los Angeles. And the pattern continues with recent immigrant groups.

As World War I (1914–1918) curtailed the stream of European immigrants, Southern Blacks replaced the immigrant populations in northern urban industrial centers in the United States, providing a needed workforce (Discovery Channel, 1993; University of Mississippi, 1994). Southern Blacks left their rural southern US roots and, like external immigrants, migrated to what seemed to be better opportunity.

In the decade between 1910 and 1920 the largest internal peacetime migration in the United States occurred. Referred to as the Great Migration (Discovery Channel, 1993; University of Mississippi, 1994) this event layered internal migration with external immigration. Rural Southern Blacks left the agrarian South and migrated to escape racial segregation, poverty, and the loss of agricultural jobs due to mechanization. Many sought out opportunities in Atlanta, Baton Rouge, Birmingham, Memphis, and Savanah, but also migrated to Baltimore, Chicago, Detroit, and Los Angeles. Southern Blacks clustered in dense neighborhoods defined not by ethnicity but race.

Urban areas in such cities as Baltimore, Chicago, Philadelphia, and New York were established and maintained sometimes by covenants that curtailed where Blacks could live, but also, to some degree by self-selection and necessity. Historic neighborhoods were created, populated by Southern Blacks who, in turn, raised families that stayed within these established boundaries. Federal desegregation resulted in further segregation as "White flight," a phenomena wherein White people moved out of urban areas to suburbs, concentrated Blacks and existing immigrant populations into ethic, racial, and economic communities in urban centers.

Forced segregation resulted in the establishment of tightly knit Black communities in many US cities. In the late 1960s, these concentrated areas of urban centers were called "ghettos." "Ghetto," often perceived as an African-American term but also encompassing other ethnic and racial groups, refers to an economically distressed urban neighborhood populated by ethnic and racial minority inhabitants. (As Midwesterners, Margaret-Mary and Ty have often discussed how some Minnesotans refer to Minneapolis as having a Red Ghetto that is almost exclusively First American.) "Ghetto" evolved from an Italian word from the Venetian dialect, *ghèto*, which was an area of Venice where Jews were forced to live in the 1500s (Domonoske, 2014; Merriam-Webster, 2015).

As Margaret-Mary and Ty purposefully began this chapter describing urban education as a distinctive context, the intent was to clarify the elements that typify urban teaching. Careful not to oversimplify, reduce, or stereotype the urban environ of education in the United States, both authors want to stress that urban education is not and should not be synonymous with or a code term for schools, communities, or districts that educate poor children of color. Both authors perceive urban education as signifying rich communities of culture, vibrant speech islands, unique circumstances, and sources of diversity that are strong and valued. Teachers simply need to be prepared to face these circumstances and challenges.

As teacher educators, Margaret-Mary and Ty, like other researchers (Darling-Hammond, 2014a and 2014b; Howard & Milner, 2014; Milner & Lomotey, 2014) view urban education as a well-defined field of inquiry and practice. Preparing teachers to teach in urban environs calls for specific skills sets, cultural frames of reference, responsive and sensitive pedagogical practices (Gay, 2000 and 2010; Howard, 2003), and carefully structured and sequenced teacher education programming. Academic Service-Learning as a teaching method strives to incorporate an aspect of community need and involvement embedded into existing coursework in a mutually beneficial, reciprocal relationship.

The notion of being "profession ready" as described by Coffman and Patterson (2014, p. iii) is a level of preparation that equips novice teachers to assume responsibility for culturally responsive teaching within urban education. This involves possessing deep subject matter knowledge as well as methods and approaches to teaching—pedagogical knowledge—in addition to racial, cultural, and political knowledge (Howard & Milner, 2014). Simply put, the knowledge teachers possess as well as their beliefs greatly impact learning opportunities for students.

WHAT LITERACY SERVICE-LEARNING FIELD EXPERIENCES LOOK LIKE

Given the unique and often distinctive needs of many urban elementary children, communities, classrooms, and schools in regard to literacy, literacy service-learning field experiences are a pedagogical pathway intended to prepare pre-service teachers to teach in urban schools. There is not a specific formula to these kinds of experiences and components, however commonalities exist. Margaret-Mary and Ty have identified four essentials that mark quality literacy service-learning field experiences for elementary teacher education candidates.

First, service-learning experiences and components are based on a community need for increased access to literacy, such as access to children's literature, improved writing, or increased reading comprehension. The need can exist within a classroom, within a school, within a school system, or within a community.

Second, the need matches a critical community need-area among pre-service teachers to become more knowledgeable about literacy content such as writing instruction, decoding, or use of quality children's literature. Or, the need may match pre-service teachers' demand for increased pedagogical content such as the importance of reading fluently to children whose first language is not English, or assisting with a community writing project, or teaching children how to access information via the Internet.

Third, the subsequent embedded literacy field experiences in teacher preparation coursework must address racial, cultural, and political knowledge that teachers should acquire. This racial, cultural, and political knowledge will better equip them to understand urban teaching and learning, confront existing beliefs, and expand the pre-service teachers' cultural frames of reference providing them with knowledge that will prepare them for the realities of urban teaching.

Last, opportunities for both orientation to a field experience site and reflection about what is being learned are requisite. As with all service-learning experiences, when pre-service teachers confront their beliefs, structured orientation to a site is necessary. Reflection opportunities support knowledge building about one's teaching craft and address the dissonance between how one was taught to read and one's literacy experiences. This is a critical component of the literacy service-learning field experience.

Carefully structured, literacy service-learning experiences can address the dissonance between pre-service teacher education candidates and urban education contexts by engaging the pre-service teachers in experiences that expand frames of reference while simultaneously providing a reciprocal benefit to community partners. Service-learning assists with authentic application of knowledge—content, pedagogical, and racial, cultural, and political knowledge—from the classroom to the community, including learning to work within an urban context (Boyle-Baise, 2002; Boyle-Baise & Sleeter, 2000).

EMBEDDED CASE STUDIES AS EXAMPLES

Based on Butin's (2003) cultural and technical conceptualizations of service-learning, the two authors' cases presented in this chapter provide a dual conceptualization of literacy service-learning appropriate for urban educational settings. Technical implementation concerns related to such issues as locating suitable partners, securing placements, logistics when a site is in another state, and addressing partnerships are highlighted. In addition, pre-service teachers' increased awareness, understanding, and recognition of diversity are also addressed. Finally, Zlotkowski's definition of a service-learning partnership is a "relationship that calls for significant investment of time and effort on both sides, relationships designed to continue far beyond achieving specific tasks" (2007/1999, p. 73).

Case 1

In this case, the partnership was formed when The Children's Charter School, one of the oldest charter schools in Baton Rouge, approached Louisiana State University's Center for Community Engagement, Learning, and Leadership seeking assistance with elementary students who struggled with reading. Margaret-Mary was contacted as a teacher education faculty member and a service-learning scholar (Sulentic Dowell & Bach, 2012).

Preparing pre-service teachers to teach reading in urban environments requires more than traditional academic methods and traditional field experiences. This site allowed Margaret-Mary the option to view service-learning as a pedagogical path to more appropriate teacher preparation. When the opportunity presented itself in 2009 to work with a local charter school, she perceived a new partnership as a way to recommit to both social justice teaching and service-learning (Sulentic Dowell, Barrera, Meidl, & Saal, 2015).

Initially, Margaret-Mary was reluctant to consider a charter school as a field site. While charters began as a means of offering choice to students and families, what transpired post–Hurricane Katrina in Louisiana colored her perspective. However, a sustained commitment to the community and providing pre-service teachers with a placement that offered them an opportunity to work inside an urban charter school prompted her to reassess her personal views and political perspectives.

Over the course of eight semesters and four academic years, Margaret-Mary and the school's instructional specialist forged a deep understanding of each other's needs, especially the school's unique need in terms of addressing reading comprehension among first graders. As well, the needs of the pre-service teachers were also kept at the forefront (Sulentic Dowell, Barrera, Meidl, & Saal, 2015).

By the fall semester of 2011, the partnership was well-established. The two first grade teachers contacted Margaret-Mary often via e-mail, for example, to request more time in their respective classes for structured small group experiences in addition to the one-to-one assessment and tutoring pre-service teachers provided. The two first grade teachers also requested an orientation meeting at the beginning of the semester to help orient pre-service teachers to the demands of teaching in an urban school, the specific developmental levels of teaching literacy to first graders, and the community aspects of Children's Charter (Sulentic Dowell, Barrera, Meidl, & Saal, 2015).

These two events were extremely important, demonstrating that the partnership had evolved to reflect a significant change and an authentic partnership. The first grade placement was an ideal fit; both the service and the learning were mutual. Involving the school's entire first grade (two sections) was an optimal experience; placing pre-service teachers in the same grade facilitated observations, interactions, and the opportunity to concentrate on the specifics of one grade level in terms of using appropriate literacy assessments, age appropriate materials, and responsive pedagogy, a rich experience for pre-service teachers' literacy field work.

What began as a simple tutoring assignment extended into providing the school's first grade team with in-depth literacy assessment case reports for each child tutored which were shared with families, often used to secure additional 504 accommodations, and functioned for some children as the intervention needed for supplemental support services (Sulentic Dowell & Bach, 2012; Sulentic Dowell, Barrera, Meidl, & Saal, 2015).

When service-learning partners share concerns, commit to one another, and are willing to dialog openly, a partnership is fostered, nurtured, and sustained. The combination of an experienced educator who knew how to marshal the resources of pre-service teachers, such as utilizing them for additional small group interaction, and a principal who allowed for teachers' decision making equated to better educational access for elementary students, a social justice concern (Sulentic Dowell & Bach, 2012; Sulentic Dowell, Barrera, Meidl, & Saal, 2015).

Student reflections illustrated the dispositional change of many pre-service teachers. Typically, after the first visit to the school, pre-service teachers expressed apprehension about working in an urban public school and expectations that the site would yield wild classes, behavior issues, chaos, a dilapidated and disorderly site, and that the teachers and administration would lack compassion and empathy.

Pre-service teachers had limited experience in public schools but often parroted media reports as their information source about public urban schools. Language such as "these students" or "these kids" permeated initial reflections and indicated a form of "othering" (Sulentic Dowell & Bach, 2012; Sulentic Dowell, Barrera, Meidl, & Saal, 2015).

Assumptions based on pre-service teachers' parochial or private schooling experiences resulted in an initial dissonance of experience, complicated by the pre-service teachers' race, gender, and income levels, predominantly White, middle income females, a demographic not reflected in the student population at Children's Charter wherein the student population was predominantly Black, and where most students came from low income households (Sulentic Dowell, Barrera, Meidl, & Saal, 2015).

Often, the medial reflection revealed shifting dispositions among pre-service teachers. Class discussions centered on feelings of guilt and some confusion about what they were experiencing, leading to deep class discussion about media portrayals of public schools in Baton Rouge. This led to class discussions focused on White privilege, private schooling, and public schools.

While some pre-service teachers were reserved and hesitated to engage in such discussions, defending their backgrounds and families as "hard working" and "middle class," subsequent class discussions provided a safe space to discuss their expanding cultural frames of reference. Pre-service teachers began to view poverty, not race, as a societal issue (Sulentic Dowell, Barrera, Meidl, & Saal, 2015).

By final reflections, concerns about chaos and uncaring teachers had evaporated and were replaced with comments about the cleanliness of the school and the willingness of the two first grade teachers to go the extra mile to assist their students. Through structured reflection activities—initial, medial, and final reflections as part of class assignments—pre-service teachers explored and grappled with their assumptions and beliefs (Sulentic Dowell & Bach, 2012; Sulentic Dowell, Barrera, Meidl, & Saal, 2015).

Through reflections, pre-service students also wrote about equity issues and how education was an equalizer of sorts. In final reflections, some questioned the equity of standardized tests being forced upon public school children in the state, realizing their private schools did not mandate tests (Sulentic Dowell, Barrera, Meidl, & Saal, 2015). This growing awareness mirrors Milner and Lomotey's discussions of teachers needing to possess racial, cultural, and political knowledge (Howard & Milner, (2014).

Case 2

Cultural competence is the acquired set of knowledge and skills needed to operate in settings that are culturally, linguistically, racially, ethnically, and socioeconomically diverse. This case also highlights a partnership, one between an urban charter school in Louisiana and a private, small, liberal arts institution in Wisconsin.

Ty's impetus for a service-learning course was a direct result of the lack of diverse field experiences in the teacher education program at St. Norbert College in De Pere, Wisconsin. While Ty acknowledged that the current field experiences had value, pre-service teachers did not have a true context for urban schools, charter schools, and schools where the racial, ethnic, and cultural diversity differed from their own experiences with school. In order to provide a unique experience for upper class pre-service teachers, Ty redesigned a unique service-learning literacy field experience focused on social justice (Sulentic Dowell, Barrera, Meidl, & Saal, 2015).

Ty also found a partner urban charter school, but it was located over 1,200 miles away in New Orleans, Louisiana. The partnership was between undergraduate students enrolled in a course entitled "Developmental Reading and the Language Arts" at St. Norbert and an urban charter enrolling 250 children which took place during a three-week January interim session.

The three-week course's service-learning format provided students with an opportunity to teach, tutor, and learn about themselves as emerging teachers while working in a public charter school for two weeks. The third week of the intersession took place back in the Midwest where students engaged with course content and reflected deeply on their experience.

In addition, while in New Orleans, Ty's pre-service teachers were challenged to live outside of their day-to-day sphere of community as a means to develop cultural competence and multicultural awareness. They lived in a Catholic Worker's residence, often four to a room, used only public transportation, and budgeted for and ate communal meals (Sulentic Dowell, Barrera, Meidl, & Saal, 2015).

In this case, pre-service teachers' notion of community was unique to the school site. Pre-service teachers were forced to compare their experiences between how and where they were raised to what they hoped to expect or expected in Louisiana. There was great intersection between pre-service teachers' reflections on *wanting* to teach in an urban setting in the future and being inquisitive to learn more *about* teaching in an urban setting. The dissonance of experience surfaced repeatedly in reflections and discussions.

In both pre- and post-reflections, pre-service teachers discussed how much they learned regarding literacy instruction. However, despite the growth regarding cultural competence, pre-service teachers were still consumed with their ability to be effective teachers. Pre-service teachers, through this experience, were forced to develop an increasing awareness of what knowledge, skills, and dispositions it would take to be an effective teacher in an urban environment that differs so markedly from their own schooling experiences and frames of reference.

Pre-service teachers were able to identify personal skills such as empathy, patience, and compassion associated with culturally competent teachers (Ladson-Billings, 1994). Becoming culturally competent is a process; removing pre-service teachers from their comfort zone was one way to create opportunities for these pre-service teachers to understand and deconstruct cultural competence. However, Ty recognizes that one course and a two-week immersion service-learning literacy field experience were not adequate in challenging the personal life experiences that led to developing beliefs about urban teaching (Sulentic Dowell, Barrera, Meidl, & Saal, 2015).

While these two cases are situated in unique contexts, two urban sites in Louisiana, they offer implications for how carefully crafted literacy service-learning field experiences can be structured to the mutual benefit of both partners. Community need was the impetus for both service-learning experiences. In addition, the need at both schools matched critical developmental needs among both groups of pre-service teachers—to become more knowledgeable about literacy and effective literacy instruction.

In each case, the service-learning literacy field experiences embedded teacher preparation coursework and addressed issues of racial, cultural, and political knowledge that pre-service teachers should acquire. While it was an initial foray, at least for the pre-service teachers, Margaret-Mary and Ty believe a series of carefully sequenced service-learning medial field experiences would better equip pre-service teachers to understand urban literacy teaching and learning, while expanding pre-service teachers' cultural frames of reference and providing them with knowledge that will prepare them for the realities of urban teaching.

Opportunities for orientation to each field experience site occurred in these brief cases. Reflection about what was being learned was requisite and the opportunity to reflect on that learning in a safe environment, where pre-service teachers could question and confront their existing beliefs, was a critical component in each of the literacy service-learning field experience cases as well.

In these cases, the authors have attempted to illustrate how deep subject matter knowledge as well as methods and approaches to teaching—pedagogical knowledge—as well as racial, cultural, and political knowledge as suggested by Howard & Milner (2014) were all woven into literacy coursework.

In this second chapter, the authors defined a current, working definition of urban education, drawing upon several of the field's most respected researchers (Darling-Hammond, 2006a and 2006b; Howard & Milner, 2014; Kozol, 2006). This working definition included an historical picture of immigrant experience in the United States that lends itself to understanding the context of urban education. Chapter 2 also contained descriptions of what service-learning field experiences focused on literacy can entail, offering two case studies from their own literacy, teacher education, and service-learning work.

The next chapter provides an overview of the goals of teacher preparation as an integral part of teacher education programming using the urban context as a backdrop. The authors suggest teacher education as a field should begin to redesign medial field experience partnerships that revolve around literacy, advocating for the establishment of a service-learning framework for field experiences. Community needs are addressed as well as what steps to take when cultivating partners and establishing placements.

3

CONSIDERATIONS WHEN CULTIVATING PARTNERS AND ESTABLISHING FIELD EXPERIENCE PLACEMENTS

One of the distinguishing features between a traditional literacy field experience and a literacy field experience with an embedded service-learning component is the placement. *Where* students are placed and *why* they are placed at particular sites are key questions instructors should take into account when considering service-learning literacy field placements.

If the service-learning component is congruent with and complementary to the pedagogical approach that frames the course or if the service-learning component is embedded within the course as a key experience, then the field placement for students is intentional and not simply an addendum to the course or scheduled out of convenience. The placement is a result of responding to a community-defined need and a relationship with a community partner in tandem with the literacy preparation needs of pre-service teacher education candidates.

GOALS OF TEACHER PREPARATION

The ultimate goal of teacher preparation is to enable teacher education candidates to enter the profession as capable, knowledgeable, and competent professionals. The training of teachers is of paramount concern—as a means of furthering a democratic society and as an economic driver. Education programs need stellar candidates and the ability to craft programs that produce high-quality educators.

Field experiences have a long-standing tradition in teacher preparation programs. As an integral part of a well-designed, comprehensive program of study and teacher preparation, field experiences, especially literacy field experiences, are carefully and intentionally structured to support, validate, and extend course concepts and course ideas; field experiences must be closely aligned with course goals. Pre-service teachers need a diverse set of rich experiences embedded in coursework in order to develop deep content knowledge about literacy as well as appropriate pedagogical literacy strategies.

As teacher educators and service-learning scholars, Margaret-Mary and Ty espouse Darling-Hammond's call for "a common, clear vision of good teaching that permeates all course work and clinical experiences" (2006b, p. 6). This vision includes coherency across a program structure. Literacy programming is a crucial component within teacher education programming. Darling-Hammond's seven features, first discussed in chapter 1, are required in order to adequately prepare teachers for twenty-first-century classrooms.

The goal of teacher education encompasses standards of professional practice built on knowledge of children that includes a deep understanding of social, cultural, and political contexts as well as the requisite content, curricular, and assessment knowledge advocated by Milner & Lomotey (2006). Carefully selected and scaffolded field experiences that are closely connected to coursework are a key element in teacher preparation. In particular, medial field experiences should be carefully designed as they are the preparation bridge between initial exposure and the final experience of student teaching.

As teacher educators invested in cultivating medial field experiences for pre-service teachers, the work of rethinking the traditional field experience is necessary. Districts and principals desire first-year novice teachers to have more and better preparation time in the field, more contact hours with students across developmental levels, and more time to develop the craft of teaching. This demand from the field is coupled with the growing shortage of highly qualified and effective teachers in many urban environs.

RETHINKING PARTNERSHIPS

In most teacher preparation programs, faculty members have a pulse on what occurs in local schools and have relationships with local educators, oftentimes at the school level. Teacher education faculty might know a principal in the district or specific teachers because of long-standing personal relationships or by virtue of the alumni base. These relationships could be defined as one of convenience or one-way partnerships.

What the authors label as a *convenience* or *one-way partnership* is quite common. For example, a faculty member teaching a reading intervention course may know a teacher at a particular grade level at a particular school or a number of teachers at various schools. This faculty member may engage in a series of e-mail exchanges or may have a face-to-face conversation that informs the teacher(s) of the course of the faculty members' need for the pre-service teachers enrolled in the course. The faculty tells the partner the number of hours the pre-service teacher needs, and what the pre-service teacher needs to do.

As a result, the faculty member sets up the partnership using already established, convenience relationships to fill the needs for the course. Convenience or one-way partnerships are often times intended for pre-service teachers to "get time in the field."

Conversely, the authors have labeled a second, more comprehensive *reciprocated partnership* as a partnership that would have a much higher degree of intentionality wherein the faculty member knows the desired outcomes for the course, has researched the community or partners, and is aware of community needs particularly as they relate to literacy instruction, assessment, and intervention. Ideally, the community partner would establish the need first. As a result, the faculty member and the community partner, which may not be school- or classroom-based, engage in intentional discussions regarding the need and the outcomes for the course, and together decide on the best course of action to move forward.

Literacy-based service-learning field experiences move the thought process from partnerships of convenience to partnerships of intentionality. Margaret-Mary and Ty have relied on partnerships of convenience or one-way partnerships. However, they would never categorize such experiences for pre-service teachers as "service-learning." On their journey toward a mature view of teacher preparation, both have come to identify literacy service-learning field experiences as optimal preparation.

In Ty's first year as a faculty member, she taught a reading assessment and intervention course. The key facet of this course was the field experience. Pre-service teachers each needed a specific number of hours in the field, an emergent reader to assess, and were required to provide interventions. As a first-year faculty member, finding a school site in a new locale, the Upper Midwest, was difficult. Locating a site that would open its doors in the middle of the day was even more difficult.

Ty grappled with interrupting the school day for local children, with her need for preparation, and with being new to the greater Green Bay area and not having established relationships. As a result, Ty relied on a faculty colleague to suggest a principal and a school site. The colleague's recommendation was needed and pre-service teachers where able to master the outcomes of the course. But the placement lacked depth; it was a one-way partnership based on convenience.

COMMUNITY NEEDS

Oftentimes in teacher preparation programs, knowledge of community needs is based on school, district, state, or even national data sets. However, there is a difference between perceived needs and actual needs. To gain a deeper understanding of the community need as it relates to literacy requires more in-depth analysis of the community beyond schools. This requires ongoing partnerships with community-based and nonprofit organizations that serve the community. By engaging in conversations or by using document analysis of such sources as income and literacy levels for communities, a more detailed picture of real community needs emerges.

For example, in Wisconsin, Achieve Brown County utilizes experiences from various sectors to improve health, safety, and education from cradle to career (Achieve Brown County, 2015). The data they make available helps to paint a picture of the needs in the community and schools. Ty has used the data provided by this organization to get a sense of the number of those living in poverty, of families and young children in the surrounding community, and of the homelessness rate of families with children, as well as diversity growth patterns.

Ty uses this data to gain deeper insight into the districts within the county and in tandem with literacy research she conducts, can draw conclusions regarding what literacy challenges a district or school may grapple with in her area. By accessing this kind of data, she is able to more accurately negotiate with local partners regarding how best to meet needs. This data also assists her when describing local need to the pre-service teachers enrolled in the literacy courses she teaches.

CULTIVATING PARTNERS

Utilizing a preestablished center on campus can be an ideal first step to cultivating partnerships, particularly those outside of school-based placements. In recognition of their civic and academic missions, 240 US colleges and universities have earned the Carnegie Community Engagement Classification as of 2015 (Carnegie Foundation for the Advancement of Teaching, 2015). Margaret-Mary has relied on her institution's center for partnership referrals. However, faculty-initiated partnerships are the most common. Regardless of how partnerships are initiated and established, cultivating sustainable partnerships takes time.

Many partners that have accepted volunteers, interns, or pre-service teachers in the past bring their memories to this new or redefined relationship. There are some partners that will be very welcoming and allow the partnerships to develop as the course takes places. Some will be more flexible with bumps, twists, and turns. However, there may be partners who desire to have everything planned from beginning to end. Regardless, Margaret-Mary and Ty have learned in this work to suspend judgment.

First, and foremost, get to know the prospective partner and become familiar with their needs. Beyond their needs, know the partner's mission, vision, and assets. The following questions are important to consider when seeking sustainable partners:

- What role does this partner play in the community?

- What are the current initiatives or programs occurring as a result of this organization?
- What need does the partner perceive?
- Does the partner understand the difference between service-learning and community service?
- Has the partner worked with your institution or department before? If yes, what do you know about the relationships?

Cultivating partners means that you have to understand the partner's needs. Cultivation also means communication and connection. If a previous partnership existed, consider that past partnerships may have not been as successful. Apprehension to enter into a partnership may exist. On the other hand, the partner may have had a very successful partnership in the past. The partner may look to you to be exactly like the previous partner. This knowledge is unknown unless cultivation occurs. Yes, prior to agreeing to the partnership, there should be more than an e-mail exchange. A partnership is a relationship.

As service-learning has grown over the last twenty years into a legitimate field of research and has been identified as a high-impact pedagogical practice, many institutions of higher education have funded centers dedicated to service-learning, community engagement, or community-based research on their campuses. Accessing these university centers for engagement can be a first step to gaining a deeper understanding of who may have interest in cultivating a partnership.

The First Meeting

The first meeting is not about the "pitch," it is about learning and establishing honest, open lines of communication and building trust. Consider having an initial meeting at the potential partner's site and not in your office or at a university campus. Travel to the partner site with the intention of learning about the partner, what they do, how they do their work, whom they serve, and their goals and mission. This initial meeting is your chance to ask a lot of questions and listen. An initial meeting is also a time and place to secure all contact information, community partner logistics, hours, and services.

Oftentimes, community partners are excited to have visitors and to share their story and show off their facilities. At first meetings, you will hear how the partner articulates the community need. You will probably meet key personnel as well. As you get to know more about them, you are able to discern if this will be a good fit. If there isn't a fit, be honest and open.

Margaret-Mary was once contacted by a community partner that wanted to use phonics instruction as the sole afterschool intervention program. She simply explained that while she understood the partner's desire to use a phonics program, that wouldn't serve the pre-service teachers she was teaching regarding literacy. She gently declined the offer to partner. If you determine that you are not the best fit for that community partner, honestly explain your rationale for not partnering and, as a professional courtesy, consider directing them to someone that will meet their needs.

Subsequent Meetings

These follow-up meetings are opportunities for sharing the course goals, defining the service, and determining the mutually beneficial nature of the partnership. In subsequent meetings, roles and responsibilities are established, negotiated, and solidified. Both partners should discuss and determine the role the community partner may want to assume in preparing students for the service and educating students about the community context and need.

Subsequent meetings are excellent spaces in which to negotiate the logistical issues, such as who is served, where activities will be scheduled, and duration in terms of time frames. Memorandums of Understanding (MOUs) can be created at subsequent meetings.

A simple MOU would include both partners' names, key personnel, partnership site address, and personnel contact information. Such an MOU would also include the scope of the partnership in brief terms. Both partners should sign and archive such an MOU.

Most importantly, the methods of ongoing communication are established in subsequent meetings. A communication memo can be helpful in determining who and how to communicate when a situation arises at the site, what communication between students and the community partner, if any, should look like, and communication methods in case of emergencies such as weather or lockdowns. A communication memo would simply explicate how communication will occur including frequency and/or duration.

Death by Meetings

Institutions of higher education are rife with meetings that are not always outcome-oriented. As you continue to cultivate your partnership, be mindful that meetings are important but they don't have to be frequent. In other words, establish a clear purpose for any meeting. Having outcome-driven meetings with set agendas, specific goals, and action steps allows your community partner to understand that you value their time and your time. Prior to asking for a meeting with your community partner, consider the following:

- Why are we meeting? What is the stated purpose?
- As a result of the meeting, what will be the next steps or action steps?
- Which partner is the most logical choice for an action step?
- Versus a meeting, is there an equally effective way of communicating the information that still allows the relationship to remain strong and intact?

FROM PARTNER TO PLACEMENT

Once a relationship has been cultivated and the partner identified, the shift in nomenclature occurs. The partner is now the placement site for the literacy-based service-learning field experience. It is at this juncture that the teacher educator has to think about the intersection of service-learning pedagogy and the literacy content of the course.

Establishing a placement for pre-service teachers does not have to be difficult as long as the logistics are clear and negotiated. But before negotiations can occur, the most important question to consider prior to establishing or agreeing to enter into a partnership is the following: Will this placement ensure that relevant and meaningful service occurs where pre-service teachers' learning is enhanced?

While service-learning work is about responding to and meeting a community need, developing pre-service teachers' ability to engage in sound literacy instruction is also of importance. Relevant service applies to responding to the partner's need but also takes into account what pre-service teachers are doing as a means of engaging in current, sound literacy practice. Meaningful service also assumes that the service will lead to measurable outcomes. As the faculty member along with the community partner gain a clear sense of what will be accomplished, how that accomplishment will be measured is significant.

Throughout this book we discuss reciprocity, the hallmark of true service-learning partnerships. Responding to a community-defined need does not mean forsaking pre-service teachers' learning. There should be discussions on how your pre-service teachers will benefit academically from this experience. In this case, the academic benefit is their development as literacy teachers.

As literacy and service-learning scholars and researchers who have developed service-learning courses for various undergraduate courses, the one service-learning experience aspect Margaret-Mary and Ty want community partners to understand is that pre-service teachers need extended time to work with students to be able to develop their lesson planning expertise using a "gradual release of instruction" model. Their expertise as literacy scholars allows Ty and Margaret-Mary to make very intentional decisions about the partnerships to cultivate and the type of placements for pre-service teachers.

At the medial field experience level, Margaret-Mary and Ty do not want pre-service teachers to merely observe, nor do they want pre-service teachers working with adult learners, because their ultimate goal is to become competent elementary teachers. Similar to classroom teachers' employment of developmentally appropriate practices, the same mindset is used with determining fit of partner and placement. Pre-service teachers themselves, depending upon where they are in their development or in the program, help to determine the placement fit as well.

While it is acceptable that the placement is not a school-based setting, there has to be a fit between the community partner's needs and course goals. Margaret-Mary and Ty have learned over time that placement and partner are not synonymous. The partner may be great, but the placement may not be a good fit for pre-service teachers and vice versa. All of the service-learning elements should be negotiated when solidifying the placement.

For example, we would welcome a community partner such as a school-based aftercare program that wanted pre-service teachers to work with elementary-aged children operating at different developmental levels on various literacy tasks such as increasing reading and writing skill. It would also be acceptable if a community center partner was seeking literacy tutoring for pairs of young children or groups of elementary-aged students or working in a one-on-one configuration. Another example of an acceptable placement might be a local community library that was seeking pre-service teachers as read-aloud volunteers.

When establishing placements, it is acceptable to be a visionary. Being a visionary means considering placements outside of "traditional" settings where literacy learning may not be apparent. Literacy learning can occur anywhere, in churches and faith-based settings, within community centers, even at community health clinics where elementary-aged children may accompany family members to appointments. Wherever the actual placement is situated, key tenets to remember are:

- Are pre-service teachers responding to a real community need that has been defined by the community partner?
- Are pre-service teachers engaged in meaningful and relevant service where their literacy content learning is enhanced?
- Are pre-service teachers engaged in meaningful and relevant service where their teaching skill is enhanced?
- Are pre-service teachers engaged in meaningful and relevant service where their pedagogical skill is enhanced?
- Are pre-service teachers engaged in meaningful and relevant service where their cultural and political capital is enhanced?
- Do the service site and activities align to the context and the outcomes of the course?

If you answer yes to these questions, the issue of *where the placement occurs* diminishes. The placement can occur in a library, community center, or even a group home. Most important is a fit between a community partner's need and the goals and needs of pre-service teachers to become more competent, more knowledgeable, and more aware of the cultural and political forces that shape urban teaching. Ultimately, increased community engagement is the goal of a literacy service-learning field placement and relationships matter.

In chapter 4, the authors present three important issues that surface in service-learning partnerships. Specifically, chapter 4 includes a discussion of literacy coursework in teacher preparation programs, mutually beneficial need, cultivating collaboration between partnerships and finally, ways the authors have successfully promoted communication and commitment.

4

COLLABORATION AND COMMITMENT

As literacy scholars, teacher educators, and service-learning practitioners, Ty and Margaret-Mary embrace the notion of teacher education as a means of social justice achieved through well-prepared teachers. Pre-service teachers who experience teacher preparation consisting of conscientiously constructed courses with service-learning components engage in authentic, meaningful preparation. This is particularly important for urban education given its challenges.

Such courses within teacher preparation programs provide pre-service teachers opportunities to think deeply about issues surrounding literacy acquisition and access for their future students. Issues such as race and ethnicity, culture, social power positioning, privilege, and politics are at the forefront. The authors posit that teacher preparation programs can intentionally foster collaboration and commitment by addressing the very issues that challenge urban education.

In the era of dubious educational reform, fueled by commercial interests, literacy teaching and teacher education have not been easy routes. This is especially true considering mandates that have required scripted curricula, shifting standards, misuse of standardized testing, and other reform strategies that mark today's political bickering around and within the educational literacy landscape. Returning again to Darling-Hammond (2010a; 2010b), Schools of Education and Colleges of Education that prepare teachers have an obligation to strengthen teaching through cohesive programming that confronts these challenges in meaningful ways.

Simply put, teacher preparation impacts teacher effectiveness which directly influences student learning and outcomes (Darling-Hammond, Holtzman, Gatlin, & Heilig, 2005). Service-learning provides a space where teacher educators can expose pre-service teachers to social issues that impact literacy learning while also providing authentic experience. As well, service-learning addresses community needs while deepening both understanding of community and enhancing civic engagement. This kind of programming promotes community collaboration and subsequent commitment to this kind of teaching.

A hallmark of service-learning is the notion of a mutually beneficial need between community partner and an entity providing service; pre-service teachers learn course objectives through active engagement (Allam & Zerkin, 1993; Conrad & Hedin, 1991; Furco; 1996; Root, 1994 and 1997; Tai-Seale, 2001). With teacher education courses, when objectives are matched to the mutual benefit of both service provider and service recipient integrating service *into* the course, deep learning occurs. As a pedagogical method to achieve authentic academic goals (Billig & Furco, 2002) service-learning engages pre-service teachers in activities that extend their lived experiences, connecting theory with practice.

To cultivate, foster, and encourage sensitivity toward the cultural mosaic typically represented in urban education, teacher education for the twenty-first-century demands coherent, relevant, culturally responsive theory, culturally sensitive pedagogy, and authentic experiences throughout the entire teacher preparation sequence (Barnes, 2006; Cochran-Smith, 2000; Darling-Hammond, 2006a; Larkin & Sleeter, 1995; Milner & Lomotey, 2014; Mason & Schumm, 2003). Unwavering commitment to children's learning and to communities fosters collaborative practice, conveying to pre-service teachers their role in improving society.

In many urban contexts public, social, and educational services vary in funding and openness to partnering with institutions of higher education. Teacher educators cannot tap into every service and meet every community need. Intentionality and selectivity in *who* the partner is and where the placement occurs is admissible. As stated in the previous chapters, literacy service-learning field experiences are not intended to compromise the academic learning and content development of pre-

service teachers. Rather, they are intended to deepen preparation, especially preparation to teach in urban schools and communities.

The efficacy of incorporating service-learning into teacher education
coursework has been well-established (Boyle-Baise & Kilbane, 2000).
Because service-learning is a robust pedagogical method connecting
meaningful, course-embedded service with academic learning goals, individual growth of pre-service teachers becomes a focus, as well as
fostering community engagement and responsibility. The mutually beneficial aspect of service-learning promotes understanding, cultural sensitivity, and knowledge about communities. In essence, both partners
benefit from the service-learning experience, with a cyclical benefit to
pre-service teachers.

As stated previously, typically, traditional field-based teacher education programs position service as an *addendum* to students' coursework,
what can also be labeled as a *convenience* or *one-way field placement*.
Literacy field experiences that integrate service-learning *within* the
course (Sulentic Dowell, 2008 and 2009; Villegas & Lucas, 2002), described as a *reciprocal placement*, result in a more sustained commitment to urban teaching. In this model, the initial awareness pre-service
teachers gain grows over time, becoming an ingrained philosophical
approach. Thus, such experiences impact pre-service teachers' orientation.

Teacher education programming is enhanced and enriched in terms
of appropriately preparing pre-service teachers to teach successfully in
urban environs by creating coursework that focuses on meeting the
needs of elementary-aged children by delivering strategically focused,
intentional service-learning components. This kind of coursework allows pre-service teachers to gain competence and confidence as literacy
teachers. In turn, the service-learning experience provides pre-service
teachers with experiences in cultural, linguistic, and economic diversity.

Courses with embedded service-learning components carefully
matched to course goals influence pre-service teachers' dispositions
which results in improved classroom practice (Boyle-Baise, 2002; Tai-
Seale, 2001). Because service-learning pedagogy is a method to address
the tensions created between urban elementary-aged students and pre-
service teachers in urban settings when lived experiences differ dramat-
ically, service-learning pedagogy diminishes the gap between students
and teachers by engaging university students in course-embedded,

structured opportunities that, through scaffold experiences, widen perspectives.

Simultaneously, such service-learning experiences not only synthesize course objectives through experiences, but also provide a reciprocal benefit to service recipients. Service-learning activities embedded in coursework can help pre-service teachers to internalize course objectives by deepening content knowledge. The authors believe that intentional teacher education programming that includes service-learning develops teacher identity, teaching philosophy, and orientation toward teaching. In essence, these experiences can shape pre-service teachers in positive ways.

LITERACY COURSEWORK IN TEACHER PREPARATION

Typically, teacher preparation programs require elementary education majors to take a minimum of two literacy courses, excluding children's literature courses which are often taught as survey courses. The nature of these courses differs greatly from program to program and expectations of accreditation agencies. However, Margaret-Mary and Ty have noted a pattern in learning outcomes outlined in their syllabi as they have taught a range of literacy courses at the undergraduate level.

In a traditional literacy course with a field-based component there are two types of learning outcomes. The first type are content outcomes which may include differentiating between approaches to phonics instruction, analyzing the differences in phonics-based versus balanced-reading approaches, or analyzing the difference in orthographic patterns between emergent and independent writers. Content becomes a primary focus, which is not a bad thing but is potentially a reductionist approach to teacher education programming in that content becomes privileged in terms of a learning hierarchy.

The second type of learning outcomes prevalent in many literacy courses for elementary majors are performance outcomes that involve producing a product related to content knowledge. Examples include developing a vocabulary lesson plan using tier 2 vocabulary, demonstrating knowledge of a particular lesson design format, mastering administration of a *Concepts of Print* or similar assessment, or analyzing data from a running record and creating a subsequent data-driven instructional plan. While both kinds of outcomes are important, they are not indicative of the body of expertise pre-service teachers should acquire.

Literacy-based service-learning field experiences are unique within teacher education. Literacy as a discipline or content area is foundational in nature and a basis for other content or disciplinary areas such as social studies, math, and science. When service-learning as an instructional practice is part of the fabric of a literacy course, a new and different learning outcome emerges. The third type of learning outcome is directly aligned to the service and corresponds to a community defined need. This third kind of learning outcome relates directly to Howard and Milner's emphasis on knowing the racial, cultural, and political environment as a teacher (2014).

Additionally, this third type of learning outcome corresponds to pre-service teachers' personal and dispositional growth in relation to children, teaching, learning, and the microcosm represented by a community. These learning outcomes may include: reflecting on cultural competence and personal growth, describing how the experience supports the community and builds on community assets, and defining their role as an advocate for equity.

The three distinct learning outcomes that drive a literacy-based service-learning field experience necessitate strong collaboration between community partner, faculty, and pre-service teachers. The role of the faculty member becomes one of a culture builder. The faculty member is responsible for fostering a positive classroom community with the pre-service teachers enrolled in the course but also with the community partner. The collaborative relationships are complex in nature, but the faculty member is now responsible for building and cultivating multiple relationships. Relationships to consider include:

- Faculty–Pre-service teacher;
- Community partner–Faculty;
- Faculty–Students;
- Students–Pre-service teacher; and
- Pre-service teacher–Community partner.

Ty and Margaret-Mary find that balancing collaborative relationships is not always easy but when there is a synergistic relationship, the service-learning field experience is beneficial to all parties involved. Strong collaborative relationships lead to strong course evaluations and advancement in Margaret-Mary and Ty's faculty roles. Pre-service teachers grow as culturally competent literacy educators, community partners are able to expand an existing service or build something new, and clients or students experience growth, motivation, and excitement as readers, writers, and literacy learners.

CULTIVATING COLLABORATION

Service-learning, teacher preparation, field experiences, and literacy instruction each have a sociopolitical implication, which is strengthened when all four of these are combined. Hence, collaboration is salient to service-learning and its success as a pedagogical approach. The role of faculty members is even more important in such a model.

It is the responsibility of the faculty member to analyze implicit and explicit power and privilege assumptions from those who are part of the collaborative process. For Ty and Margaret-Mary, this responsibility is at the forefront of any service-learning field experience. Service-learning implies incorporating a social justice frame as does literacy learning and teaching in general. Social justice is not impressed upon others but fully reflected in the actions and choices of the faculty member as well. A danger includes unintentionally promoting attitudes of noblesse oblige or savior mentality in pre-service teachers (Boyle-Baise, 1998).

When entering the collaborative relationship, Ty and Margaret-Mary reflect on their own privilege and power positions. They seek out ways to authentically unpack the salient identities such as gender, racial, ethnic, economic, and educational positions. As faculty members working with pre-service teachers, community partners, and students, it is important to recognize how these identities inform the collaboration and create hierarchies where some may have more assumed power or privilege than others. As teacher educators, they openly address these issues with pre-service teachers.

The questions then are: how do teacher educators engage in collaborative partnerships when the collaborators have different experiences and viewpoints towards education and have a different investment in the community? How do teacher educators incorporate community need in a dignifying manner? A teacher educator who is committed to serving the needs of the community and who strives to prepare pre-service teachers as adequately as possible will always have to struggle to identify whether a partnership is an authentic collaboration or a convenient collaboration as well as to recognize the potential unintended consequences of a literacy service-learning field component.

As service-learning teachers and scholars, one framework to consider is what Delano-Oriaran (2012) calls an authentic and culturally engaging (ACE) service-learning model. The ACE model is grounded in asset-based thinking and cultural competence. The ACE model frames collaborative partnerships from all levels to ensure the community is being served and that pre-service teachers are developing in their own cultural competence and social justice advocacy. Collaborative partnerships on the front end may include the following communication as facilitative of collaboration at each of these levels.

Community Partner–Faculty

- Initial face-to-face conversations
- Communication memos
- Memorandum of understanding

Faculty–Pre-service Teacher

- Inclusion of the service-learning experience in the syllabus
- Lectures/demonstrations to frame the service experience
- Opportunities to learn about the community partner
- Orientation session to ease pre-service teachers into a site
- Opportunities to reflect about ongoing service-learning experience

Students–Faculty

- Introduction to pre-service teachers and your role
- Getting to know names, interests, and literacy needs
- Understanding community and position of community partner with community

Students–Pre-service teacher

- Providing concrete ways to build relationships first
- Having clear expectations for interactions and safety

Pre-service Teacher–Community Partner

- Having a clear understanding of the communication process or chain of command
- Knowing the services the community partner provides and their commitment to the urban environ
- Understanding expectations of professionalism

This list serves as a catalyst for readers to consider the intricacies and nuances of collaboration and commitment demanded by literacy service-learning field experiences. The intention of this list is to be realistic and to note the difference between an authentic collaboration and a convenient collaboration, and why faculty may be drawn to one over the other.

Service-learning has limitations, as it functions within the confines of academic institutions such as the academic calendar and available resources, and the potential to foster what the literature terms a "savior mentality" toward teaching (Butin, 2003). Many community partners are able to be flexible but there are some that may not have the same level of flexibility. In moving from collaboration to commitment there has to be honesty about what you can and cannot provide to the community partner and an awareness of the generally messy nature of teaching.

Finally, Ty and Margaret-Mary acknowledge service-learning is complicated and complex work and not meant for all teacher educators. Service-leaning demands a knowledge base and a commitment to community, civic engagement, and social justice. It is involved and difficult work. While the authors believe that commitment to community, civic engagement, and social justice coalesce around literacy learning and teaching, teacher education, and service-learning, they admit it is a model and frame that works well for them but one that has been honed over time and with practice.

PROMOTING COMMUNICATION AND COMMITMENT

Relationships exist because of the commitment that is present and the reciprocal nature of the relationship. Commitment in service-learning is more than a mere "yes." It is about the level and methods of communication and trust (Potter, 2002). As with any relationship, the partnership relationship that exists between service-learning partners is established and nurtured through communication and trust. Considering these communication pathways in advance is important.

While no formula exits, open communication must take place and be accommodated. For any relationship to have positive outcomes, there must be open lines of communication. Communication can take many forms and there is no set form that is most advantageous. It can be informal and organic or it can be formal and structured. Margaret-Mary favors an informal communication style wherein either partner reaches out to the other, typically through e-mail or phone calls, when a need rises. Ty prefers a more structured communication style where set times for communication and predetermined issues are set for discussion. Both communication styles are valid and both work.

Formal approaches to communication may include a MOU that outlines the responsibilities of the community partner, pre-service teachers, and faculty. Other formal communication opportunities may take the form of interval check-ins via e-mail or face-to-face communication. As it is ongoing throughout the experience, the check-in serves to address any issues both partners may anticipate.

As a service-learning scholar, moving your classroom outside of the predictability of the traditional classroom is rich and rewarding. The goal is to learn with and in the community. Thus the commitment is not only between the community partner and the teacher educator but also between pre-service teachers and the community, involving a high level of commitment and communication.

As partnerships are fluid and evolving, the same is true for communication and commitment between all members of a partnership. This is especially germane considering that most universities are on a quarter or semester system. Thus, while pre-service teachers rotate through quarter systems or semesters, community partners and faculty are static. This calls for renewed commitment and rebuilding of trust each semester.

Trust is one way to secure a commitment and develop an authentic partnership. The sustainability of Margaret-Mary's partnerships and service-learning placement sites are a result of shared honesty and authenticity. When meeting with her community partner she willingly shares her commitment to urban literacy education through her personal experience. She does not leave her story up to interpretation but is very straightforward.

Margaret-Mary also shares her journey in becoming a teacher, her role as an assistant superintendent, and the impact that Hurricane Katrina has had on her life. The sharing of the story is not for entertainment but it helps to connect and build bridges with other people involved in the work of literacy learning and urban education. As an educated White female, she seeks ways to connect to partners, establish rapport, and build trust in urban communities where she may appear as an outsider because of her race and education level. She has learned that communication and commitment are vital attributes.

Ty has learned similar yet distinct lessons on her journey to becoming a service-learning practitioner. She relates the process of her professional development in becoming a teacher via an alternative route—Teach for America, her return to higher education to build more knowledge about teaching and learning through advanced degrees, and the impact that being a highly educated teacher has had on her life. As an educated Black female, she has often had to work very hard at not being viewed as an outsider because of her advanced level of education. Ty has learned that communication and commitment are essential qualities.

In chapter 5, the authors address the ways literacy-based service-learning field experiences are organized and managed. This next chapter will also provide concrete ways to ensure logistics and risk are addressed as ensuring a safe and effective learning environment for all.

5

ORGANIZING AND MANAGING A SERVICE-LEARNING FIELD EXPERIENCE

Organization on the front end of any collaborative experience is a certain way to ensure success. Starting early, revealing the needs of both partners, sharing schedules and calendars, establishing timelines, deciding on supervision, instituting communication methods, as well as discussing the parameters of each experience, are all steps that can lead to organized, coherent, and optimal experiences for both partners and participants. And despite any pre-planning, situations will arise and the unexpected will occur.

Managing the logistics, the relationships, and the unexpected during the service-learning field experience is absolutely necessary. Literacy-based service-learning field experiences in urban settings require a higher level of organization and management. As service-learning practitioners and literacy scholars, Ty and Margaret-Mary have found their organizational methods have contributed to the success of each of their service-learning field placements and have maintained the long-standing relationships they have with community partners.

The goal of this chapter is to provide insight into the organizational structures utilized to ensure both the success of pre-service teacher education candidates and that community partners are adequately served. It's important to note that no foolproof formula exists, however, the authors share what has worked for them in several settings with different partners. They underscore the pre-planning needed to ensure a successful experience for all involved.

SUPPORTING SERVICE-LEARNING: PRE-STEPS AND FIRST STEPS

Service-learning is a high impact practice that many college and university teacher preparation programs have embraced. Different institutions have rewarded service-learning as a pedagogical approach and scholarly endeavor in various ways. As a teacher educator in a university or college setting, knowing the resources available to support your service-learning field experience is valuable to the organization needed on the front end of the experience.

Pre-steps

As an initial pre-step, any teacher educator who makes the decision to embark on a service-learning literacy journey should first take a personal inventory of the literacy course they want to select for inclusion. Examine your reasons for wanting to incorporate service-learning. How will a service-learning component impact course goals? How will a service-learning course fit with the sequence of courses in the teacher education program? Are there programmatic issues to consider?

Next, another pre-step for teacher educators considering service-learning should be to ascertain if their college or university has a vetting process. For example, at Margaret-Mary's institution, Louisiana State University (LSU), an application and syllabus is submitted to a standing university committee. Once approved, a course is listed as a service-learning course, designated by a "SVL" classification, on all course schedules as well as on student transcripts. At LSU, the university committee meets once in fall and once in spring semester, so submissions for approval can take time.

At Ty's institution, St. Norbert College, there is a Director of Academic Service-Learning. The faculty member in this role is responsible for sending the call each semester to faculty interested in acquiring the community engagement tag (CENG) as part of the course. Faculty submit their syllabi and a short application. The Academic Service-Learning Advisory Committee, which is composed of actively engaged service-learning practitioners and scholars, evaluate course syllabi. However, once a course has a CENG tag it does not automatically transfer to the next semester nor is this tag coded on a student's transcript. The faculty member must resubmit an abridged application each semester for consideration.

Finally, teacher educators need to determine if any approval is required from direct supervisors. For instance, do directors and/or deans have to approve such a course? This pre-step may seem like a compliance step, but it is important to also understand how direct supervisors view service-learning. Margaret-Mary once experienced a lack of support from a former director and a former dean (not an educator) who stated openly that all field experiences are service-learning. She has also enjoyed the near unanimous support of other directors and deans.

First Steps

If you are tenure track faculty, it is crucial to investigate how service-learning is viewed and recognized at your institution. Attempt to address your institution's mission language versus tenure and promotion policy, noting if community-engaged activities are or are not reflected adequately in tenure and promotion. Taking the time to examine existing policy and documents can help bring to light the tension between what the institution says it does versus what it rewards faculty for doing. The tension between policy and practice should be examined and those interested should ask direct supervisors to provide recommendations regarding tenure.

Some institutions both recognize and reward community-engaged scholarship (CES), an umbrella under which service-learning belongs. If your intuition supports CES, locate official definitions of scholarship/ faculty work, criteria for review, and examples of supporting documentation in tenure and promotion guidelines for review. The percentage of effort should be reflected in what faculty does. The weight to be accorded each will be consistent with the department's mission and with the faculty member's job duties and work assignments. Discovery— scholarship—needs to reflect the value of engaged research and teaching activity.

The tension between university policy versus university practice needs close examination; changing the culture *will* impact practice. If your institution does not recognize and reward community-engaged scholarship, gather support in like-minded colleagues, and develop and suggest clear definitions of what constitutes community-engaged scholarship, community-engaged teaching, and community-engaged service. A faculty member's experience in scholarship and teaching should assure that he or she will bring intellectual and educational values to the university and the broader community.

In addition to knowing your institution's stance on CES and service-learning, acquaint yourself with what your institution can provide in terms of support for service-learning discovery and teaching. Margaret-Mary and Ty were both service-learning faculty fellows at their respective and former institutions. A fellows program helped to bring awareness to each of them as to what services their institutions provided to support service-learning course development as well as what funding was available to support course redesign and service-learning research and scholarship.

The authors understand that funding opportunities vary by institution. However, the faculty fellows programs were valuable because all faculty involved were invested in redesigning courses or creating service-learning experiences. Ideas were shared and readings were required to lay a foundation regarding service-learning theory and pedagogy. The support system of working with colleagues across campus was valuable to both authors.

As a reader of this handbook, for those individuals at the early stage of incorporating service-learning field experiences embedded in a literacy course, involvement in a service-learning fellows or reading group can be an important first step in organizing the field experiences at the course level and building a knowledge base. A fellows program or reading group may help you in thinking through the following:

- What are the literacy needs of the children in my urban community?
- What community partners may I consider reaching out to in order to learn more about their work, contributions, and needs?
- What are the nonnegotiable learning outcomes of my course?
- What are the negotiable learning outcomes of my course?
- What support can I expect from my unit, college, or university?

Organization in the idea stage can be highly supported if the structures are in place, however, a fellows group or reading group is not absolutely necessary. As described in chapter 1, Ty had not gone through the faculty fellows program prior to redesigning a literacy course to include her first urban-based service-learning field experience. She was aware of needs in post-Katrina New Orleans and reached out to a community partner with which she has a personal relationship. The initial partnership started out of convenience but developed into a reciprocated partnership.

Ty's knowledge and understanding of service-learning pedagogy and scholarship was fostered because another scholar directed her to Margaret-Mary's work in literacy and service-learning in post-Katrina New Orleans. She then embarked on a personal study of service-learning. Professional organizations such as the American Educational Research Association and the Literacy Research Association both have special interest groups and study groups that examine community-engaged scholarship, service-learning, and literacy. Ty capitalized on what the field had to offer, and her personal learning was rich and professionally rewarding.

ORGANIZING THE EXPERIENCE

Once you have attended to the pre- and first steps, a next step in organizing any service-learning experience is seeking out and developing a relationship with a community partner. There are numerous books and studies on building relationships with the community and community-engaged learning (see chapter 10 for books found useful). Campus Compact (2015) and the resources they provide can support a novice service-learning practitioner.

However, a literacy-based service-learning field experience has nuances of its own because most teacher education programs have logistical expectations or requirements informed and shaped by accreditation agencies. These relationships are even more distinctive when the service-learning field experience is specific to the development of elementary literacy teachers in urban environs. As stated earlier in this chapter, knowing how program leaders and direct supervisors view and recognize service-learning is requisite to implementing a service-learning component in a literacy course.

There are many possibilities and ample opportunity to enjoy a strong reciprocated relationship that meets a community-defined need. And, an effective urban service-learning field experience does not have to take place in a K–12 school setting (see chapter 7 for alternative placements and partnerships). The faculty member must keep at the forefront a clear understanding of the course goals, what pre-service teachers are expected to know and be able to do by the end of the course, and how these requirements meet community partner needs.

After a community partner is identified and a relationship is established, it is important that the faculty member and community partner are clear on how the need may be addressed and what each party is able to contribute. For instance, course objectives for a developmental or early literacy course for pre-service teachers may include:

- Examining effective approaches for decoding, vocabulary, and word attack skills or strategies,
- Demonstrating an understanding of how language and language learning are meaning-centered and that the teaching of language must occur in contexts that are meaningful,
- Creating print-rich environments that reflect community and familial assets, and
- Incorporating [state] writing standards for early grades K–3 into lesson design.

In this instance of an early literacy course for pre-service teachers, communication with the community partner is invaluable. The faculty member must discern how elementary literacy content knowledge will inform the service-learning field experience and vice versa. The community partner's needs can then be embedded into course goals, enriching and extending the original course.

UNDERSTANDING AND DEFINING COMMUNITY NEEDS

The intention of literacy-based service-learning field experiences is to promote elementary teacher candidates' understanding of urban contexts and how their actions as teachers can impact the community. Utilizing service-learning as a means of expanding opportunities for developing elementary pre-service teachers means that the service-learning experience serves as a "text" that is interpreted and analyzed to develop, increase, and improve pre-service teachers' learning about effective elementary literacy instruction. The text is the community and the specific need to which pre-service teachers are responding. Thus, the faculty member must know and understand the text prior to assisting pre-service teachers' understanding of the community text.

Within service-learning, understanding about community is inextricably aligned to course goals and outcomes (Bringle & Hatcher, 1996; Furco, 1996; Zlotkowski, 2007). This knowledge building requires time to augment students' fund of community knowledge (González, Moll, & Amanti, 2005) with an asset-based mindset (Dweck, 2006). Keep in mind that this serves as a model for how pre-service teachers will also build knowledge about new communities they may encounter as novice teachers. The understanding may be specific to a course and community, but the lesson is universal. Community then, becomes an important component of all teaching and is emphasized through service-learning.

Pre-service teachers may study maps of the community to understand housing and school boundaries. Historical documents can be accessed and may help shape an understanding of the community as well as fostering a deep understanding of the community partner, its strategic goals, and funding sources. Teacher candidates may even conduct interviews to gain community perspectives as they relate to literacy needs aligned to the course. Margaret-Mary once included community literacy narratives about family gardening in a literacy course that included a service-learning component establishing community gardens.

The following vignette illustrates how Margaret-Mary incorporated service-learning into an existing literacy course and how she also structured assignments that allowed pre-service teachers to gain understanding about community. The vignette also demonstrates the transformative nature of a carefully crafted literacy service-learning component for pre-service elementary teachers.

Vignette: The Garden Project (Sulentic Dowell, 2008)

In this elementary literacy course, community gardens were established at a local elementary school. The gardens became a catalyst for many learning experiences for the school's children. The city where the university was located and where this study was conducted reflected the de facto segregated education system found throughout the southern United States; White students typically attend either private, Christian-based "academies" or public county schools located in "White flight" communities surrounding urban centers while Black students predominantly attended public city schools.

Margaret-Mary set expectations and provided pre-service teachers with a demonstration of what she expected from them when on site in the school's gardens. That meant she dressed for gardening, interacted with staff and students, and she participated fully in planting, weeding, dead-heading, and harvesting the gardens. Margaret-Mary took great care to ensure that school and community center schedules coincided with university schedules.

As a means of assisting pre-service teachers' understanding of this community, they visited homes and collected literacy narratives about family gardening practices. This assignment resulted in pre-service teachers involved in the Garden Project learning a great deal about the community in ways that traditional assignments could not yield.

Often, comments surfaced during class discussions that illustrated how pre-service teachers' dispositions were shifting regarding the students and communities with whom they were interacting through the Garden Project and epitomized the reciprocal, mutually beneficial nature of the embedded service-learning experience. Reflections also yielded data that illustrated how the service-learning experience was transformative.

One pre-service teacher continually expressed her gratitude for the opportunity to work in the school gardens; she shared how this experience was more helpful to her than any other practicum field experience, as she was "forced" to examine her own belief system and feelings. Service-learning was extremely valuable for this student who, like so many others who participated in the Garden Project, became knowledgeable about social, economic, and linguistic difference. Thus, the literacy service-learning experience allowed pre-service teachers to internalize course goals and objectives, and to examine how their personal belief systems are shaped by their world views.

This vignette, culled from a study reported in 2008, illustrates the level of organization, commitment, and communication needed for successful service-learning experiences. It is important to note that Margaret-Mary worked with the same school and community center for five consecutive semesters.

While this level of organization may seem more like content delivery, having a deep understanding of the community supports pre-service teachers in their development as civic-minded teachers. In Ty's literacy-based service-learning course, the students in her class conducted their field experience in New Orleans, not in the greater Green Bay community. Their knowledge building was accelerated and at times seemed distant and disconnected from what was happening in her classroom in Wisconsin. Some pre-service teachers struggled to grasp the importance of learning about a "new" community; some were resistant. Others were curious.

As a result, it was incumbent for Ty to not only build students' understanding of New Orleans as an urban environment, but also to help pre-service teachers understand the historical context of the city. To accomplish this, Ty's had a geographer from her institution, the literacy specialist from the service site, and other community members serve as guest lecturers to help contribute to students' understanding of the community beyond the actual school campus. The lesson learned was the efficacy of knowing a community in which you eventually teach.

CONSIDERATIONS: UNDERSTANDING TEMPORAL FEATURES

There are several components that teaching faculty must consider when organizing and developing a framework for a service-learning field experience. The needs of community partners differ. What works and "fits" at one site can differ greatly from what is effective at another, even if the proximity between sites seems negligible.

Time is a consideration and should be discussed with the community partner. This includes both contact time and travel time. If young children are "dropping in" to a site, arrival times can be inconsistent. If accessing children at a school site, time frames may be short and must be adhered to strictly. Travel time to and from the site also has to be considered. Traffic in an urban area can be unpredictable. For Margaret-Mary, each semester, she spends class time discussing routes, carpooling, and parking. In the past, she has even organized class caravans so pre-service teachers can arrive prepared and on time.

However, these logistical questions may vary by each college and university setting. As faculty some questions to consider are:

- Will the service-learning field experience span the whole semester or only part of the semester?
- Will the service-learning field experience occur during course meeting time or outside of the course meeting time?
- As the instructor do I have to be present at any, all, or some portion of the service-learning field experiences?
- Are there forms or background checks that may be needed prior to engaging in the service-learning field experience?
- Does a university/college's risk management policy come into play?

Because many community organizations may not operate on the same time schedule as college or university timelines, knowing and communicating how long the service-learning field experience will take place must be discussed. Local school schedules often do not match university and college schedules. High stakes testing may curtail visits to school campuses as well. If there is intentionality about responding to a community need, then a candid conversation regarding the time limitations is necessary. What to consider discussing regarding timelines may vary but below is a list of some issues:

- How long is your semester, quarter, or trimester?
- How long will students be able to commit to being at the site?
- When will students be able to start and when will they need to complete their commitment, particularly in order to allow time for reflection or sharing of how the community need has been met?

MANAGING SERVICE-LEARNING FIELD EXPERIENCE

Teacher education programs differ greatly and their institutional structures do as well. As a program that considers student teaching as required, there may be provisions made for pre-service teachers to ensure their success during a service-learning experience. Examine any institutional policies regarding personal transportation. Your institution may require transportation as part of the program, or just during student teaching. Policies may need to be reworked to include a service-learning field experience placement. Both authors have each grappled with transportation issues and have created the following questions that may assist:

- Is public transportation in the urban setting reliable and accessible from campus?
- Are there ways for pre-service teachers to get gas cards to offset the cost of driving?
- Does the institution have a relationship with the department of public transportation where pre-service teachers may be able to use transportation at a reduced cost?
- Can course descriptions and course catalogs be rewritten to explicitly include travel time and transportation requirements?
- Can handbooks and orientation to teacher education materials also be updated to explicitly include travel time and transportation requirements?
- Can lab times for undergraduate teacher education literacy courses be listed as TBA (to be announced)?

A FINAL WORD ABOUT RISK MANAGEMENT

Minimizing risk and ensuring pre-service teacher safety is of the utmost concern of all institutions of higher education. As alternative and school-based community partners are solidified, risk must be considered. Many community-based organizations have protocols to minimize risk as well. Some partners, like Baton Rouge's Volunteers in Public Schools, underwrite the cost for background checks. Other community partners expect background checks but do not fund them. As part of the planning conversations with the community partner, this should be addressed. Questions to consider:

- Who is responsible for risk management forms and protocols on my campus?

- What are the potential risks that need to be considered while engaged in the service-learning field experience?
- What are the risk management protocols for the placement site?

KNOWING YOUR INSTITUTION

College and university operations vary from institution to institution. It is important that you know what supports are available at your institution. Some institutions have an office or center of service-learning, community engagement, or civic engagement. These offices or centers can be very helpful in negotiating risk management documents or other logistical issues that may be salient to your service-learning field placement.

If your institution does not have a center or office that supports faculty in this capacity, knowing who on the campus is responsible for risk management and talking to that individual is necessary. You may find your campus has limitations on what pre-service teachers can do as enrolled students. Some faculty who want their students to have extended time in the field may want to offer the course outside of the time sequence set by the institution. Ty accessed this option and used her college's intersession for her service-learning embedded course. Time grids are regulated by the institution and there may be a formal process to offer a course outside of this structure. Know the process.

KEYS TO SUCCESS

Organization and managing literacy-based service-learning field experiences can be what may determine if an experience is successful. Organization requires a knowledge of service-learning pedagogy and best practices and what the authors call pre-steps and steps that can lead to success. Management requires a knowledge of community and your institution, including the support that may be available to help plan logistics and to ensure pre-service students remain safe as defined by an institutions' risk management office. Service-learning involves deep understanding, commitment, and a great deal of effort.

In chapter 6, the authors explicate what is meant by the medial field experience and provide a view of what such literacy experiences look like when service-learning is incorporated into them. Comparing traditional to service-learning literacy medial field experiences, the authors offer a new a new paradigm for teacher preparation.

6

EMBEDDED SERVICE-LEARNING COMPONENTS IN EDUCATIONAL FIELD EXPERIENCE

Service-learning is one method that pre-K–higher education can utilize to reimagine and redeliver teaching with a seamless transition from grade-to-grade, presented with a natural flow of educational experiences for pre-service teachers, students, and schools (Myers & Pickeral, 1997). This chapter highlights how service-learning at the medial level can be embedded within elementary education coursework, as opposed to being an add-on to coursework, an addendum to theory, or an additional aspect of a professional practice course.

The goal of teacher preparation is to create meaningful field experiences that prepare pre-service teachers for classrooms. The authors have chosen to focus their careers as teachers and researchers on urban education. As discussed throughout this book, the context of urban education calls for teachers who are equipped to teach children from urban homes, schools, and communities. For the authors, service-learning literacy components ensure that medial level field experiences are purposeful and meaningful for the community partner, the children within those sites, the development of pre-service teachers, and the faculty member as a teacher scholar.

It is important to briefly differentiate between community service and traditional field experience. Community service is one-sided. While the service provider may feel a sense of accomplishment or satisfaction, what they gain through service does not truly extend to deep learning.

In field experience, pre-service teachers are practice teaching while earning practicum hours needed for certification or licensure. This is traditionally viewed as learning how to teach, typically with a specific age group or level, and occurs with all disciplines or content areas represented in the elementary grades.

MEDIAL FIELD EXPERIENCE: BETWIXT AND BETWEEN BECOMING A TEACHER

As presented in chapter 1, traditional field experiences are a kind of experiential education for pre-service teachers to "practice" teaching. Early or initial experiences are designed to acclimate pre-service teachers to classrooms and schools, medial experiences are designed to hone teaching practice, and the capstone or final experience is a gradual release of responsibility. A key element in a field experience, especially at the medial and final levels, is the scaffolded support that pre-service teachers receive, both from preparation program faculty and partner teachers in the field.

As with every learning experience, not all individuals learn at the same pace or in the same way. This is true of pre-service teachers as well. Some enter a preparation program more ready to learn and better equipped to acquire content knowledge and pedagogical teaching skill. Some pre-service teachers possess life experiences that allow them to acquire racial, cultural, and political knowledge as described by Howard and Milner (2014). Elementary education pre-service teachers must acquire disciplinary or content knowledge from literacy, math, social studies, and science, typically from the first grade through fifth grade level, within their program of study.

The scope of this book is focusing on the medial level field experiences, where pre-service teachers enter this phase of professional development with approximately two semesters of preparation before they student teach. They often see themselves as students, not pre-service teachers. Jaquith best describes field experience as program contact hours with children often associated with methods courses where pre-service teachers learn methods of teaching literacy, math, social studies, and science (1995).

While all field experiences are important, the quality and depth of the medial field experience influences the quality of the final field experience which directly relates to the level of preparedness of pre-service teachers to become competent novice teachers.

TRADITIONAL MODELS OF MEDIAL FIELD EXPERIENCE

Traditional models of medial field experience generally follow two methods of delivery. One model involves a field component attached to each content methods course. Typically, content courses are blocked, with literacy usually paired with social studies in one block of courses and math and science blocked together. In literacy, for example, if a program contains two literacy courses, both will usually be taught as corequisites, and both will have a field experience component. Another model clusters or blocks all content courses together and offers an entire semester of field experiences in all content areas.

Little communication occurs between faculty who teach methods courses. To compound the lack of communication between field experiences, quite often a separate office of personnel arranges the field experiences. Further disconnect occurs when additional coursework is blocked with content methods courses, sometimes classroom management, often special education coursework, and other required courses such as assessment and planning, are scheduled in addition to content methods courses. Some require field experiences while others do not.

These two methods of field experience management do not reflect nor even resemble Darling-Hammond's clarion call for "a common, clear vision of good teaching that permeates all course work and clinical experiences, creating a coherent set of learning experiences" (2006b, p. 6). Rather, in both models, there is little common vision that binds coursework together and as a result, learning experiences are disconnected and incoherent.

THE DANGERS OF DISCONNECTED MEDIAL FIELD EXPERIENCES IN PROFESSIONAL PRACTICE COURSES

As teacher educators, there has been astonishment expressed between the authors about the disconnect and lack of cohesion in teacher education programs of which we have been a part. Neither Ty nor Margaret-Mary experienced a cohesive program when they initially sought their teacher education degrees.

It is the role of both faculty and program coordinators to find the balance between building content knowledge regarding effective literacy instruction and pedagogical knowledge, and to consider ways to provide field experiences that are connected to courses and within courses. Often racial, cultural, and political knowledge building is ignored or is only applicable when pre-service teachers are enrolled in multicultural education or social inequalities courses. Given the importance of preparing teachers for urban contexts, teacher education faculty need to reimagine how they deliver content learning and develop pedagogical skills as well as how they address the role of racial, cultural, and political knowledge that impacts teaching and learning.

This is a bleak picture. For the authors, it's as if the preparation of teachers has become stuck in time, not changing since the two of them received their initial preparation. But both authors believe that service-learning is a pedagogical pathway that can bring cohesion and connection to teacher preparation, especially when considering literacy and urban settings.

EMBEDDED SERVICE-LEARNING AT THE MEDIAL LEVEL: A NEW PARADIGM

Literacy service-learning field experiences hold the promise of redefining teacher preparation by offering more authentic preparation within a context that is connected to teacher education coursework, providing a more realistic view of the challenges of teaching, and matching community need to the content, skills, and dispositions teachers need to acquire. Instead of simply focusing on one content area, like traditional field experiences, service-learning field experiences are more comprehensive in nature and can commingle content in a more unified manner.

Literacy service-learning field experiences offer learning opportunities for pre-service teachers that intersect literacy with other content, that include multiple instances to use expansive pedagogical skill, and that are connected to the development of the dispositions pre-service teachers need in order to offer culturally responsive and culturally sensitive teaching. Instead of working and learning in isolation, often in classrooms that try to simply accommodate pre-service teachers into already established routines and sequenced lessons, pre-service teachers are welcomed as pre-professionals within the learning community.

As an example, when Ty decided to redesign her literacy course, refining and refiguring it to address a community need in New Orleans and to enhance civic learning outcomes and strengthen campus-school-community partnerships, she was able to combine content learning with pedagogy and dispositions. The following vignette illustrates how pre-service teachers under her tutelage gained valuable content knowledge about literacy learning but also gained skill and expertise in pedagogy, cultural knowledge, and political issues. The vignette also illuminates how logistics and communication are essential.

Vignette (The Morris Jeff Experience, 2015)

Ty was concerned that so many of the pre-service teachers enrolled in her literacy course had limited experiences with non-White, economically disadvantaged students. She felt strongly that teacher education programs have the responsibility to develop cultural competence in pre-service teachers so that they may understand the diversity of students in their classrooms. She knew that for pre-service teachers to better understand the needs of the children they might serve, they needed greater cultural competence skills.

The impetus for a service-learning course was a direct result of the lack of diverse field experiences in the teacher education program in a small town in Wisconsin. To provide a literacy service-learning experience for upper class pre-service teachers, Ty applied for an institutional-based grant to plan and work with an urban charter school in New Orleans for two weeks in January, and she redesigned her course, "Developmental Reading and the Language Arts," to include literacy, social justice, and service-learning. An overarch-

ing question guided this work: What dispositions did students identify as the most needed to be successful in diverse teaching settings?

The partner urban charter school was located in New Orleans,
enrolling 250 students from pre-K to grade 5. Ty and the pre-service
teachers traveled over a 1,000 miles to engage in a service-learning
experience while immersed in the community. The triangular partnership between teacher education, the charter school, and the student affairs division at St. Norbert had been developed over five
years. Nuances of this literacy service-learning experience included
student leaders/teaching assistants (TAs) who previously participated
in the course, an application/interview process, and a semester-long
preparation for students and TAs developed and carried out by student affairs professionals. Through this experience, pre-service
teachers specifically gained literacy content knowledge to use data to
differentiate reading instruction in general education classrooms.

The three-week course's service-learning format provided students with two weeks of concentrated time to teach, tutor, and learn
in a public charter school in New Orleans. The final week, back in
the Midwest, students acquired additional literacy content and reflected on their experience. Students were challenged to live outside
of their day-to-day sphere, shopping on a budget, eating and living
communally, traveling via public transportation. The pre-service
teachers' personal notions of cultural competence and their beliefs
were impacted. In particular, the pre-service teachers became more
adept at teaching in an urban environment.

The purpose of this study was to explore the ways in which students thought about their own cultural competence and increased
empathy for the community, displayed open-mindedness toward an
urban setting, and became more proficient in strategic literacy teaching. For instance, one pre-service teacher stated that "the urban
school setting offered me an experience to approach racial and economic diversity in [public] schooling."

After the service-learning experience, pre-service teachers indicated an interest in teaching in an urban context and preferred the
service-learning experience to the traditional course field experiences. Results indicated that this experience resulted in pre-service
teachers developing an increased awareness of the knowledge, skills,
and dispositions needed to be effective in a diverse urban teaching
environment. They identified personal attributes such as empathy,
patience, and compassion which are associated with culturally competent teachers, as Ladson-Billings discusses (1995 and 2000).

The intersection of literacy education and service-learning in an urban environment created a unique opportunity for pre-service teachers. Becoming a culturally competent teacher is a journey, and removing pre-service teachers from their comfort zones is a method to create opportunities for teachers to understand and deconstruct their ideas about culture, poverty, race, and urban existence. Ty recognizes that neither one course nor two weeks is enough personal life experience to strongly influence pre-service teachers' approach to teaching (Sulentic Dowell, Barrera, Meidl, & Saal, 2015).

The redesigning of this course underscores the potential of service-learning programs to aid in the development of culturally competent and socially just teachers (Flannery & Ward, 1999). Ty's pre-service teachers also gained valuable content knowledge about literacy learning as well as increasing their pedagogical skill. The concentrated time, two weeks, also meant that Ty was able to provide timely feedback and guidance.

One of the most difficult aspects of teaching is learning to orchestrate learning. Between preparing and designing lessons, marshaling and organizing resources, and establishing learning environments, pre-service teachers can become easily overwhelmed. Add pacing of lessons within given time frames, managing behaviors, and balancing the many demands of teaching, and the complex nature of teaching becomes apparent. In the vignette included in this chapter, Ty illustrated how she was able to connect learning in meaningful ways. The literacy service-learning experience included social learning, economics, and basic geography.

THE ROLE OF REFLECTION IN SERVICE-LEARNING

Reflection is a key tenant of both teacher preparation and service-learning. Reflection can be individual or collective but the intent of reflection is to allow pre-service teachers to think about what they are learning. Reflection within service-learning must be ongoing and intentional. It is critical for pre-service teachers to link their understanding of literacy practices and theories to their service-learning field experience (Eyler, Giles, & Schmiede, 1996). Reflection is essential to unpack thoughts, tensions, and opportunities for the future.

Reflection can be categorized within three domains: (a) knowledge of community and need, (b) knowledge of self as teacher, learner, and advocate, (c) knowledge of effective literacy instructional practices. Reflection is oftentimes teacher-directed where faculty requires students to respond to a set of questions or leaves time open for pre-service teachers to share what they learned and how it connects to course content.

When service-learning is a field experience, the reflection process may take a variety of forms such as the written journal; a video, blog, or Tweet (Twitter message); oral reflections through structured and unstructured conversations; or pictorial representations. In some cases, the reflective process may be part of a larger assignment. Capitalizing on pre-service teachers' habits, Facebook posts can also be used as reflection tools.

Ty prefers beginning and ending reflections, measuring the growth and learning after an experience. Actively engaged in service-learning as a pedagogical approach that drives the field experiences in many of her courses, the final reflection is intended to bridge theory and experience. Students are asked to reflect on a specific experience, in some cases the lesson that was the least effective or the most effective. The intent is to analyze the experience within the broader context by noting the correlations between content knowledge, planning, and teaching, and by measuring the impact of getting to know students and building authentic relationships.

SAMPLE PRE-FIELD EXPERIENCE REFLECTION QUESTIONS

Included here is an excerpt from Ty's actual syllabus. The questions were intended to both prompt and push pre-service teachers' thinking about their experiences. These were given to pre-service teachers before departing for New Orleans. She titled these reflection prompts as:

Your Learning

- What do you hope to learn while in New Orleans?
- What do you hope to learn about teaching in an urban environment?

- What do you hope to learn about students as readers and individuals?
- What knowledge to you hope to gain regarding community strengths and its relationship with schools, teachers, and families?

Dispositions

- What dispositions do you feel that you will be able to develop while in New Orleans? How and why?

Teaching

- In what ways do you think you may be challenged to grow as a culturally competent teacher, learner, and individual?
- How will you challenge yourself to remain open-minded, suspend judgment, and identify moments when you are experiencing discomfort?

Sample Post-Field Experience Reflection Questions

Ty also provided reflection prompts after students returned from their two-week literacy field experience in New Orleans. The following are again taken from her syllabus and were meant to capture students' thinking about the experience in terms of their teaching, dispositions, and personal learning.

Literacy Teaching

- Identify three things you learned in this course about using data to drive day-to-day reading interventions for elementary readers.
- Describe one challenge you encountered during your experience as it relates to the following:

  - Teaching literacy content (text-based vocabulary and comprehension).
  - Do not focus on management.

Dispositions

- What three teacher dispositions do you feel this experience helped you develop and why?

Your Learning

- What did you learn about New Orleans, public schools, and the community assets that informed your development as a culturally competent teacher?
- What did you learn about teachers who are invested in communities like New Orleans? What teaching dispositions did they portray and how did they influence your growth as a literacy teacher?
- What did you learn from students that you did not expect to learn?

Margaret-Mary employs initial, medial, and final reflection, evaluating how dispositions, content, and skills shift over time. Through reflection, she gains an understanding of students' thinking in order to understand how stereotypes, particularly around literacy instruction, are reinforced, shifted, or dismantled. From a social justice perspective, it also provides insight into how students are making meaning of their personal experience and their journey towards becoming more socially just educators.

Listed here is an excerpt from Margaret-Mary's syllabus where she explains her goals and the goals of the embedded literacy service-learning experience. She makes it explicit what the service-learning experience entails:

> In addition, this is a *designated academic service-learning course*, where your notions of civic engagement will expand as you become more involved in your local community and more knowledgeable about issues surrounding public education in Baton Rouge and Louisiana. Through enhanced field work and a required service-learning component, you will address critical community literacy needs, fostering serious examination of real-world literacy issues and concerns, which in turn encourages critical thinking about civic responsibility. Please visit the LSU Center for Community Engagement, Learning and Leadership at: http://www.lsu.edu/ccell

In addition, listed here are the three interval prompts Margaret-Mary's uses. Keep in mind that she uses reflection prompts as a way to elicit feedback about the literacy service-learning experience but also as a means to gather data about the experience. As such, they are intentionally brief and contain no leading language. Her coding and analysis reveals what each group of students finds surprising, what they have learned, and how their thinking has changed over the course of a semester. Like Ty, Margaret-Mary also focuses on literacy teaching, dispositional shifts, and personal learning through reflection.

- Initial reflection prompt: *What surprised me?*
- Medial reflection prompt: *What have I learned about myself and teaching?*
- Final reflection prompt: *How has my thinking about teaching changed?*

The form of the reflections does not matter nor does the interval at which they are captured. What does matter is that pre-service teachers are given the opportunity to think about what they are learning and to consider those thoughts through the reflection process. Reflection, then, also provides connectivity between course content and other content areas, practices, and dispositional learning.

In chapter 7, a brief discussion of the merits of alternative partners and placements is presented. Readers are also provided examples of alternative partners and placements for consideration.

7

ALTERNATIVE PARTNERS AND PLACEMENTS

Service-learning as a pathway to expand literacy learning and teaching skill for elementary teacher education is intended to respond to a real community need while simultaneously offering pre-service teachers opportunities to acquire teaching content and pedagogical skills and to develop dispositions toward teaching. To assume that the only venue for service-learning within teacher education occurs in schools is to assume that many teacher education programs do not understand the relationship between teaching and learning.

There are multiple sites outside of schools for elementary teachers to develop the content and pedagogical planning and dispositional skills needed to be effective teachers. In fact, there are many sites of learning, including but not limited to K–12 schools. In this chapter, we describe many potential alternative partners and placements for readers to consider.

EXTENDING BEYOND ELEMENTARY CLASSROOMS AS TYPICAL FIELD SITES

As authors, we believe in serving the community. We also recognize that national conversations regarding teacher preparation identify one of the weakest-perceived areas of teacher preparation as literacy. Specifically reading development has received much scrutiny. However, despite the political rhetoric that seeks to deprofessionalize teacher preparation programs, Ty and Margaret-Mary see their roles as gate-keepers to the profession. In addition to fostering sensitivity while developing competent teachers, teacher educators like Ty and Margaret-Mary address tensions that arise when preparing teachers for urban environs as part of the political atmosphere.

In the last several decades, reading has been a narrowly defined, prescriptive process in a market-driven, political climate (Altwerger, 2005; Shannon, 2001 and 2007) as both personal and political forces have intensified (Allington, 2002a, 2002b, 2004, and 2006; Garan, 2002 and 2004), dictating the kind of literacy instruction urban public school children receive. The literacy "forced" on urban children does little to create agency or provide access to societal power (Coles, 2003; Finn, 1998; Meyer, 2010).

Literacy learning for urban students is shaped by family economic status, race, language, culture, and access to opportunity. As researchers describe a longitudinal view of a US teaching force increasingly disparate from urban public school populations (Au, 2006; Ayers & Ford, 1996; Compton-Lilly, 2004; Delpit, 1995; Freedman, Simons, & Casareno, 1999; Ladson-Billings, 1994 and 1995), many in teacher education, like Ty and Margaret-Mary, have responded by focusing attention on diversity issues in literacy methods courses.

Despite efforts to address the dissonance between teachers in urban areas and the children whom they teach, a significant number of researchers continue to question whether pre-service teachers are sufficiently prepared to work with culturally diverse student populations (Barnes, 2006; Cochran-Smith, 2000; Gay, 2000; Ladson-Billings, 2000; Villegas & Lucas, 2002). Literacy service-learning field experiences can assuage this disconnect addressing the impact of culture, ethnicity, economics, and issues of access with pre-service teachers through literacy coursework (Sulentic Dowell, Barrera, Meidl, & Saal, 2015).

A decade ago in her 2006 American Educational Research Association (AERA) presidential address, Ladson-Billings reminded us of the "effect of poor education, poor housing, poor healthcare" in explaining her conceptualization of an "education debt" (p. 10). Howard and Milner (2014) and Milner and Lomotey (2014) continue to express concern over the conditions that typify urban classrooms.

While alternative service-learning partnerships outside of the traditional classroom will not completely address the issues of urban education, they do provide pre-service teachers with experiences that will challenge them to grapple with the everyday realities and complexities that inform children's literacy experiences and reading development in urban schools. Alternative service-learning partnerships are not a panacea, but they are a move toward better, more adequate teacher preparation.

EXTENDING BEYOND ELEMENTARY CLASSROOMS AS TYPICAL FIELD SITES

Alternative partners and placements outside of K–12 classroom settings allow pre-service teachers to understand that they have the opportunity to gain new knowledge and insight through the service they provide. These partners and placements may give pre-service teachers a revised perspective on what community entails and the role the community has as it relates to educational opportunities and experiences.

Alternative partnerships are a way to dismantle the power that is assumed by the K–12 educational system. These partnerships bring learning to the community and are for the community. These types of partnerships allow for the conversations related to literacy learning outside the context of test scores and school rankings. Pre-service teachers need these kinds of opportunities to gain perspective and understanding of urban teaching. These types of experiences may serve as an unintended benefit of developing cultural competency, making the service-learning experience even more vital for pre-service teachers.

Alterative partners and placement sites challenge pre-service teachers to make distinct connections between literacy learning and the community without the constructs and limitations that schools assume. Self-awareness and acceptance of differences are key skills necessary for teachers to teach students who are culturally different from themselves (Diller & Moule, 2005). In alternative sites, pre-service teachers are able develop their identities as "cultural beings" with something to learn as well as something to contribute to the community.

Pre-service teachers are on a journey to becoming culturally responsive teachers. It is the responsibility of teacher educators to walk alongside them. Culturally responsive teachers understand and acknowledge the social and cultural characteristics and linguistic abilities of their students, which may be different from their own (Gay, 2002). However, teacher educators must create the conditions for pre-service teachers to identify the ways they have been influenced by microcultures including but not limited to race, gender, economic diversity, ethnicity, age, religion, language, sexual orientation, family unit, and geographic location.

POTENTIAL COMMUNITY PARTNERS

In this section, we briefly introduce alternative partners and placements that can be considered when seeking literacy service-learning field experiences. Again, such partners and placements offer an integrated type of preparation experience combining content, pedagogy, and disposition learning.

Libraries

In many communities, libraries do much more than house books. They offer programming during the summer and on weekends when students are not in school. Many evenings, public libraries provide urban students safe places to congregate. Libraries also serve the community by supplying access to computers and to specialized documents such as test prep materials and tax prep materials.

Libraries also program literacy experiences such as read-alouds, storytelling, and family literacy events. In some urban areas, libraries ameliorate lack of literacy access. Internet access is available and digital literacy is accessible. Public libraries are a viable site for a service-learning placement.

Community Centers

Community centers in urban settings offer more than arts and crafts or open gym basketball time. These are spaces where meals may be served to ensure that children and families in the community have access to a hot meal. Oftentimes funded by private donors and federal dollars and operated as not-for-profit and nonprofit organizations, their viability/

vitality is determined by their usage. The more programming that can be offered in community centers, the more funding those centers can acquire to program events to expand existing programs. Literacy programs are often embedded in community center programming.

The literacy programs typically offered in community centers range from early childhood programs to adult literacy options. Many community centers offer family literacy or intergenerational programs designed to assist young parents and boost access to books. Community centers also offer adult literacy programs such as GED completion programs, assistance with federal forms, and learning to read and write options for second language learners as well as other adult (18+ years) populations that lack print literacy skills. Also, literacy for mentally challenged adults may be a community center offering. Internet access is typically available.

Often community centers host performance literacy events, such as spoken word competitions, attractive to adolescents and their families. Other competitions can also be a regular part of community center literacy programming such as writing contests. Book drives also take place at community centers, typically targeting other community entities but sometimes simply as a drop-off and distribution point for urban areas that do not support public libraries. Community centers are also a practical site for a service-learning placement.

Coffee Shops

The authors are not promoting Starbucks here but believe it important to mention that, in many communities, there has been an influx of small business owners who want to serve the community (and increase profits) by making coffee shops a space where community action and organizing can take place. Walk into your local coffee shop, and you may also find a bible study or a book club occurring. If the owner has identified a community need and has opened up their space to serve that need and maybe a bit of free coffee, they are also a feasible site for a service-learning placement.

Faith-based Spaces and Churches

Throughout time, churches have been hubs for literacy development. This is where many children learned to read, memorize, and recite texts. Many churches across denominations function as businesses however, at their core, they desire to serve the community. Churches that have the community-ascribed title "mega church" typically have a lot of unused spaced during the day and evenings when programming does not occur. The goal of the church is to serve the community. Thus, faith-based spaces and churches are also feasibly workable sites for a service-learning placement.

Literacy Centers

Perhaps one of the most obvious alternative partners and placements sites for literacy service-learning are literacy centers. Literacy centers are grounded in the community but oftentimes just target and serve adult learners who lack print literacy skills or who are learning English as a second language. Many of these organizations are looking to expand their program offerings or need volunteers. What the authors have discovered is that literacy centers may focus on adult learning but also offer childcare, and thus have a ready population of children who can be served. These are sites where innovative literacy practices are valued and welcomed.

YMCA/YWCA

The Young Men's Christian Association and the Young Women's Christian Association may be viewed as community centers but they have been around for years and are well-established in many urban communities. Some regional sites have close relationships with schools that are able to operate their program offerings in these spaces, allowing individuals in the immediate community to have access to their programs. They are mission-driven organizations so they are always willing to partner in ways that allow them to live out their mission. YMCA/YWCAs are also potential sites for a service-learning placement.

Battered Women's Shelters and Safe Houses

These sites are not as easy to access due to their specific intent to provide a safe haven for women and children who are the victims of abusive relationships. However, Margaret-Mary has accessed several such sites. While the logistics are tricky and safety is the ultimate concern for those who seek shelter, these sites also have a great need for books and literacy activities for children who accompany their mother. Early in her career at LSU, Margaret-Mary built a library of children's books at a local shelter. Because of confidentiality issues, pre-service teachers worked remotely, compiling and sorting books; all communications were privileged and delivery was confidential.

The center director was the contact and the provider of all information about clients. It was from the center director that a need for children's books was established. Pre-service took this limited information and began to gather books, through donations, through book order points, and from such inexpensive sources such as Goodwill, the Salvation Army, and yard sales. Pre-service teachers applied their knowledge of developmentally appropriate books for age levels three through twelve as well as being mindful of ability and interest levels. Additional readings were incorporated into course readings; statistical information was gathered about local populations.

If readers are willing to work extra hard, the benefits can be extra rewarding. Often viewed as portraits of the seamier side of society, these entities can provide a rich field experience placement that is guaranteed to raise the consciousness of pre-service teachers. Shelters are promising sites for a service-learning placement, especially for generational literacy activities.

Homeless Shelters

These sites, like battered women's shelters and safe houses, are not as easy to access as other alternative partners and placements. Most homeless shelters are gender-segregated, and in fact few shelters in most urban areas allow women and children. That kind of knowledge alone speaks volumes about what homeless women and their children face. This kind of partner/placement is a prime example of how different content areas, such as literacy and social studies, can be commingled with efforts to build literacy content knowledge, in this instance the efficacy of access to literature, while also addressing dispositional knowledge.

The following vignette illustrates how one service-learning literacy scholar intentionally sought out a local library as an alternative partner and placement. Although the pre-service teacher featured in this vig-nette was preparing to teach secondary English in middle school, the implications for elementary pre-service teachers and elementary teach-er educators are transferable. This vignette highlights the efficacy of using a library as an alternative field experience placement.

Vignette (Library as Alternative Field Experience Partner and Placement, 2013)

Jackie's journey into service-learning began with her application to Louisiana State University's faculty scholars program—a semester-long course designed to assist those faculty interested in service-learning to incorporate its philosophy, principles, and practices into one of their courses. Jackie, an English education teacher educator, began her search for potential libraries by contacting the local Head of Teen Services for public libraries. From the start, she wanted to work with a variety of libraries that served economically and racially diverse populations and wrote the following e-mail:

"I'm teaching an adolescent literature course with a service-learn-ing component. My vision is to send groups of four students to a library that serves young adults and have them work with a librarian to assist him or her with their needs in regards to teen programming, cataloging, surveying, promoting, making a display, whatever the needs might be. They would be required to spend 10 hours on this project and part of their course grade depends on their contribution to the project . . . Do you have any branches who might be interested in participating? I really want students in a variety of settings."

Jackie's contact responded:

"YAY!!! I really like the fact that you are teaching the teachers to think of public libraries as 'community partners'."

This local librarian then helped Jackie establish partnerships with three different libraries: one with vibrant teen programming; one with less-structured programming but frequent use by its patrons; and a third which served more as a holding place for adolescents after school or for non-book programming such as SAT prep courses or tutoring.

Each group of pre-service teachers enrolled in Jackie's course worked with their placement partners to design and enact differing projects based on the local public library branch's needs and reflected patrons' interests; group 1 worked with the teen group to organize and host a Battle of the Books; group 2 held weekly contests in which patrons wrote Tweets about their favorite books; and group 3 created recommended book lists and attempted to survey their patrons. But, Jackie admits, those projects did not come easily. She commented about the richness of diverse placements as being key, but she also admitted they were a lot of work.

Upon reflection, Jackie learned several lessons as a service-learning practitioner who utilized an alternative placement. She shared that it would have helped if all of the partners as well as the students had attended their first meeting with more clear and concise ideas of the types of service projects in mind. She also underestimated the need to identify problems beforehand. Assuming that the process would be more collaborative, she found herself in the uncomfortable position of having to identify for the partners what their "problems" were so her students remained engaged.

While Jackie learned the importance of sharing ownership with students and community partners, she also underestimated her role in establishing and sustaining partnerships. She learned that she must maintain frequent communication and assume a more active role in the design of what the partnership should look like. (Sulentic Dowell & Bach, 2012).

This vignette demonstrates the challenges of literacy service-learning partners and placements that are viewed as alternative. While Jackie, the author of the study featured in the vignette, admitted challenges and struggles, the experience was rewarding for the pre-service teachers involved.

In the next chapter, chapter 8, the authors share ideas for assessing literacy service-learning experiences. Included in this chapter are sample rubrics and rating scales.

8

ASSESSING SERVICE-LEARNING FIELD EXPERIENCES

Service-learning occurs at the intersection of content learning—in this case, how to be a literacy teacher—and community engagement. Through service-learning, pre-service teachers respond to a real community need while increasing pedagogical skill. Clear outcomes for coursework with service-learning components ensure that pre-service teachers can achieve the necessary knowledge, skills, and dispositions to be highly qualified and effective in the classroom. In this chapter, the authors share methods for assessing literacy service-learning field experiences.

Throughout this text, the authors have contended that service-learning field experiences are a pedagogical approach that more adequately supports teacher development versus traditional field experiences. Literacy-based service-learning field experiences have the power to provide elementary pre-service teachers with unique and impactful learning that supports knowledge building and understanding of elementary literacy practice. As authors, we have couched literacy service-learning in one of the most challenging teaching contexts, urban educational environments.

The complexity of teaching and learning means assessment can be equally complex. While measuring content knowledge may seem straightforward and assessing pedagogical skill appears uncomplicated, assessing dispositional shifts is less clear-cut. Assessment for service-learning should be authentic, valid, and reflective of content knowledge, pedagogical skill, and dispositions. Feedback is important as well. Approaching this chapter, the authors examined their own practice and considered the following questions:

- How is pre-service teacher content learning assessed and measured throughout urban service-learning field experiences?
- How is pre-service teacher pedagogical skill assessed and measured throughout urban service-learning field experiences?
- How are pre-service teacher dispositions, attitudes, and openness toward children and communities assessed and measured throughout urban service-learning field experiences?

Further, Margaret-Mary and Ty grappled with other questions such as:

- How do teacher educators know if a course is effective in supporting pre-service teacher content knowledge of effective elementary literacy practices?
- How does the service-learning field experience develop pre-service teacher ability to provide effective elementary literacy instruction?
- How can assessment strategies model effective assessment methods for pre-service teachers?

Often Margaret-Mary and Ty encounter high-achieving pre-service teachers who possess adequate content knowledge but that content knowledge does not translate to practice. They have also had experience with pre-service teachers who manage behaviors well, relate to children, colleagues, and families, but lack requisite content knowledge.

The complexity of teaching plays out in assessment. What can appear exact becomes messy and sometimes inappropriate. For example, both authors work at institutions that use Praxis test scores as measures of content knowledge, but high scores on Praxis do not equate to skillful teaching. Reducing teaching expertise to content assessment is misleading.

WHY ASSESS?

Assessing pre-service teacher literacy content knowledge, the field experience, and engaging in reflective discourse is a deliberate, intentional, and methodological process. The authors focus on assessment of student learning at the course level, assessment of the community partner relationship as it relates to the service-learning field experience, and assessment of pre-service teacher educator effectiveness as it relates to content, pedagogy, and dispositions.

When assessing service-learning field experiences, it is important to recognize that there is no single form of assessment that is best or the most accurate. As with all evaluation, a multiplicity of assessments will allow faculty to develop a complete picture of the service-learning field experience, pre-service teacher development, and pre-service teacher acquisition of course content.

WHO AND WHAT TO ASSESS

Those who employ service-learning field experiences as part of required coursework must be proactive in planning for assessments to ensure that course outcomes are aligned to program expectations. Assessing pre-service teacher performance and learning throughout the literacy service-learning field experience ensures that pre-service teachers receive the feedback they need. As a result, faculty is able to track the experiences of pre-service teachers to inform course-level revisions.

As it relates to literacy content, teacher educators at the course construction level must determine what pre-service teachers will know and be able to do by the end of the course. By defining outcomes early on, the teacher educator can have a clear vision of how the service-learning field experience will provide pre-service teachers with an opportunity to learn the academic content and develop as elementary literacy teachers. During the service-learning field experiences, teacher educators have the opportunity to observe pre-service teacher actions, provide concrete feedback, and monitor pre-service teacher development over time.

In addition to assessing the pre-service teacher, assessment data should also be collected from the community partner. The teacher educator may assess the relationship as it relates to communication, time, and the service site. The most important piece of information that may be gleaned from assessment data from the community partner is the impact of service on meeting the defined need.

TYPES OF ASSESSMENT

Assessment should be both formative and summative. Formative assessment allows for monitoring and feedback throughout the experience. Formative assessment allows faculty to make necessary changes and adjustments as needed during the service-learning field experience. The purpose of literacy-based service-learning field experiences is to enrich the reciprocal process of teaching and learning.

Summative assessment is cumulative and typically requires pre-service teachers to demonstrate knowledge through a variety of tasks ranging from multiple choice responses assessing content knowledge related to the course to open-ended essay questions or a portfolio of work. The key purpose of the summative assessment is to measure pre-service teachers' increased learning over time. Because the service-learning field experience is part of the course, it should be part of the summative assessment process.

ASSESSING PRE-SERVICE TEACHER LEARNING

When pre-service teacher learning is aligned to course learning outcomes, faculty can most effectively assess progress through assignment construction. Beyond multiple choice tests and essays to assess literacy content knowledge, diverse and distinct assignments can provide insight into pre-service teacher thinking. Additional assignments may include pre-service teacher-led discussions, digital presentations, oral presentations, and lesson designs.

Lesson planning and reflections about instructional practice are assignments that are commonly assessed in most teacher preparation coursework. Lesson planning is paramount to teacher development, but expectations vary among faculty. Depending on the placement site, developmental level of students, and the instructional expectations of the course, literacy planning components vary.

In Ty's service-learning course, pre-service teachers engaged in the course are challenged intellectually by engaging in rigorous course content. They are required to read complex texts, develop lesson plans, and reflect on their own teaching practices (Meidl & Nissen, 2015). Literacy-based lesson plans derived from student assessment data are required for students enrolled in Ty's course.

Pre-service teachers begin working with students their second day at the school site by facilitating one-on-one and small group literacy lessons. Scripted lesson plans in Ty's course mean that students write everything they will say to students, including checks for understanding through questions and explicit directions for procedures and behaviors. While this is extensive, it is necessary in order for pre-service teachers to learn to plan effectively based on data.

Scripted plans allow Ty to determine if the students are meeting the course objectives by:

- Creating data-driven lesson objectives,
- Aligning lesson-level assessment to the lesson objective,
- Including an opportunity for direct instruction, scaffolded practice, and independent practice, and
- Including opportunities for reteaching beyond oral explanations.

Oftentimes reflection is overlooked as a form of authentic assessment. However, if structured well and aligned to course objectives, reflection can be one of the most powerful forms of assessment. Reflection allows the teacher educator to peer into the thought process of the pre-service teacher. Reflection promotes analysis concerning pre-service teacher learning, and examines the shaping of personal theories and beliefs regarding effective literacy instruction.

The type of reflection can vary based on the course and the field experience. Video reflections, blogging, or written reflective papers can all be adequate types of reflections. The benefits of reflection reach beyond student learning by providing evidence for course changes and improvements for the service-learning field experience connected to the course (see chapter 7 for sample reflection prompts).

RUBRICS

The creation of detailed rubrics will allow students to focus on specific aspects of their learning and development in methodological ways. Margaret-Mary and Ty actually create rubrics with pre-service teachers. Content, pedagogy, and dispositions are all included. Pre-service teachers assist with determining what is exemplary, mediocre, and unacceptable. Rubrics can be simple or they can be complex. For instance, if written products are part of the experience, then written expression can be included on rubrics.

The rubric below is used in Ty's class as part of the self-evaluative process. Unlike many of the collaborative rubrics, this rubric was created by Ty. The intention of this rubric is for pre-service teachers to engage in self-reflection and to evaluate their own reflective process. Ty has found this to be quite helpful and informative as these reflections do not count toward a significant portion of the grade. The goal is for the pre-service teachers to display honesty and openness as part of their reflective process, rather than including what they think "Ty wants to know or hear."

Margaret-Mary uses rubrics differently. As part of her ongoing literacy service-learning field experience, pre-service teachers also tutor one-to-one and work in small groups. However, a final report of assessment and tutoring is generated and shared with school-based faculty.

Table 8.1.   Self-Reflection Rubric

My Learning Rating 1-2-3	I use my prior experiences, classes, etc., to communicate my ideas and unpack my understandings and possible misunderstandings of students in urban communities. I describe my journey as a literacy teacher and/or as a teacher in urban communities advocating for educational equity.
My Dispositions Rating 1-2-3	I critically reflect on the pre-service teacher dispositions and their value to me as a pre-professional. I focus on two to three salient dispositions that are important to me in my development as an effective literacy teacher.
My Teaching Rating 1-2-3	I reflected on the literacy methods used in my lesson. I identified the moments where I did not hold my students to high expectations and why. I critically reflected on my level of comfort and/or discomfort in teaching the literacy content or in building authentic relationships with my students.

The reports are used to corroborate what the classroom teacher is seeing. Given that working with students one-to-one is almost a luxury in an elementary classroom of 20–25 students, the need of the community partner, the school, is for individual attention.

In turn, the final report becomes an artifact of the service-learning experience but also functions as a means for pre-service teachers to demonstrate what they have learned about assessment and instruction. Each semester, the previous semester's rubric is introduced and pre-service teachers amend it as a class activity. The following are the two rubrics generated through Margaret-Mary's literacy service-learning field experience. Table 8.2 is the initial status assessment rubric; table 8.3 is the completion of tutoring (instructional) rubric.

ASSESSMENT METHODS TO MEASURE COMMUNITY IMPACT

Traditional methods of assessment to measure impact of the service-learning field experience may include surveys, interviews, observations, and reflective journals. The pre-service teacher, community partner, students, and families may complete these assessments. The goal is to know to what extent the pre-service teachers understood the community need and met the defined community need. Community partners and other stakeholders should have a role in the assessment of pre-service teachers.

Service-learning is based on relationships and reciprocity. All partners should have a sense of voice and agency throughout the process. The community partner can give input about the learning of each student as viewed through its lens. Including the community partner in assessment procedures affirms the need for honesty and openness.

There are many benefits when the community partner is engaged throughout the service-learning process. One-on-one discussions may provide the space to identify what worked and was successful, and what was not, by discussing specific examples. It is almost inevitable that a misstep will occur by the faculty member, by the pre-service teacher, or by the community partner. Through honest engagement and check-ins, a true partnership can flourish. When issues arise or mistakes occur,

Table 8.2. Assessing and Guiding Classroom Reading Instruction Initial Status Report Rubric

Excellent 13–15 points	Adequate 10–12 points	Minimal 0–9 points
Content: Includes all assessments administered with dates; fully completed and detailed background section; detailed assessment procedures and results section	**Content:** Includes all assessments administered with dates; partially completed and partially detailed background section; partially detailed assessment procedures and results section	**Content:** Includes some assessments administered with some dates; partially completed and sketchily detailed background section; partially detailed assessment procedures and results section
Concepts of Print and sight vocabulary sections complete including overall statement	*Concepts of Print* and sight vocabulary sections complete	*Concepts of Print* and sight vocabulary sections incomplete
Graded word list section complete with an example	Graded word list section complete with partial example	Graded word list section incomplete with partial example
Oral reading–silent reading–writing sections complete with 2–3 solid examples	Oral reading–silent reading–writing sections complete with examples	Oral reading–silent reading–writing sections incomplete with examples
Goals are listed using appropriate language	Goals are listed using some appropriate language	Goals are listed using inappropriate language
Dispositions: Demonstrates understanding of how language impacts literacy learning; honors dialect and linguistic difference	**Dispositions:** Demonstrates partial understanding of how language impacts literacy learning; negotiates dialect issues with student	**Dispositions:** Demonstrates minimal understanding of how language impacts literacy learning; complains about student dialect
Excellent 4–5 points	**Adequate 2–3 points**	**Minimal 0–1 point**
Mechanics: Adheres to APA; 1–2 usage mistakes and/or 1–2 grammar mistakes; 1–2 spelling and/or punctuation errors	**Mechanics:** Follows APA; 3–7 usage mistakes and/or 3–7 grammar mistakes; more than 3 spelling and/or punctuation errors	**Mechanics:** Does not follow APA; more than 7 usage mistakes and/or grammar mistakes; more than 7 spelling and/or punctuation errors
Consistently written in simple past tense	Written in simple past tense with some tense shifting	Written with lack of past tense or tense shifting throughout
All parenthetical information, bracketed information, and examples professor provided are deleted	Most parenthetical information, bracketed information, and examples professor provided are deleted	Contains more than 2 instances of parenthetical information, bracketed information, and examples still intact
Paginated/double-spaced	Paginated/double-spaced	Not paginated/single-spaced

Table 8.3. Assessing and Guiding Classroom Reading Instruction Completion of Tutoring Report Rubric

Excellent 13–15 points	Adequate 10–12 points	Minimal 0–9 points
Content: Includes list of three goals; requisite paragraphs directly correspond to and address goals; contains a recommendation paragraph that lists at least one recommendation per goal	**Content:** Includes a partial list of goals; requisite paragraphs somewhat address goals; contains a recommendation paragraph but a section is missing or partial	**Content:** Does not include all three goals; does not include paragraphs that correspond to stated goals; recommendation paragraph does not align with stated goals
Contains detailed description of what was accomplished at sessions addressing goals; clarifying examples (okay to attach samples)	Contains description of what was accomplished at sessions addressing goals; inadequate, partial, and/or sketchy examples	Does not contain description of what was accomplished at sessions addressing goals; does not contain adequate examples
Mechanics: Adheres to APA; 1–2 usage mistakes and/or 1–2 grammar mistakes; 1–2 spelling and/or punctuation errors	**Mechanics:** Follows APA; 3–7 usage mistakes and/or 3–7 grammar mistakes; more than 3 spelling and/or punctuation errors	**Mechanics:** Does not follow APA; more than 7 usage mistakes and/or grammar mistakes; more than 7 spelling and/or punctuation errors
Consistently written in simple past tense; recommendation section is in *future tense*; uses clinical language throughout	Written in simple past tense with some tense shifting; recommendation section is in *future tense*; primarily uses clinical language throughout	Written with lack of past tense or tense shifting throughout; recommendation section is not in *future tense*; clinical language is used sporadically
All parenthetical information, bracketed information, and examples professor provided are deleted; end punctuation consistently followed by two spaces; books listed by category with italicized titles; author(s) listed in a consistent fashion	Most parenthetical information, bracketed information, and examples professor provided are deleted, 1–2 examples or bracketed/parenthetical information remain; end punctuation primarily followed by two spaces; books listed by category with titles; author(s) listed inconsistently	Contains more than 2 instances of parenthetical information, bracketed information, and professor-provided examples that are not deleted; end punctuation is not consistently followed by two spaces; books not listed by category and/or with titles missing; author(s) missing and/or listed inconsistently
Paginated/double-spaced	Mainly paginated/double-spaced	Not paginated and/or single-spaced

rectify and repair the situation quickly so that relationships are not jeopardized.

Honesty is a key aspect of the partnership. Assessments where the community partner can be honest without fear of judgment are key. Assessments received from the community partner should create a space for a partner to be upfront about their concerns and about how difficult or challenging situations were handled, and to provide constructive feedback regarding the experience and the pre-service teachers. Collection of this data may take place at a meeting, conversation, or through a more formal evaluation form.

In summary, because literacy service-learning field experiences are so unique, no one type of evaluation can adequately assess learning or the impact of the service-learning experience in meeting the community need. However, the areas of content, pedagogy, and dispositions should all be included. As teacher educators, reminding ourselves of the developmental aspect of becoming a teacher is helpful. Growth over time and multiple ways to assess progress are important constructs to include.

Please see the works cited section, which is a compilation of all references used in this book. While some are recent, many others are seminal in nature and are regarded as key citations.

The service-learning resources section (appendix) is designed to support the reader in their journey as a literacy teacher educator becoming a service-learning practitioner scholar.

SERVICE-LEARNING RESOURCES

This section was designed to support the reader in their journey as teacher educator, literacy teacher scholar, and service-learning practitioner scholar. Many enter the role as teacher educator because of a personal love of learning and a desire to advance the rigor and professional reputation of the teaching force. Those who are literacy teacher scholars have a deep passion for and knowledge of literacy and possess the breadth of knowledge and expertise it takes to be an effective teacher of early and emergent readers.

As service-learning teacher scholars, the foundation as a literacy scholar and teacher educator was necessary for both authors. They answered an innate call to serve the community, learning from the community, and they challenge pre-service teachers to do the same.

Those engaged with this work will find that there are many resources in each of the respective areas represented in this chapter. The construction of this chapter is the result of Margaret-Mary and Ty's engagement in deep reflection about their journey and what brought them to this work and the mentors on-the-page that continually influence, refine, and redefine their teaching and scholarship in the area of teacher preparation, literacy learning, and service-learning.

The resources presented are organized into four distinct and divergent sections. The first section focuses on the theory and historical underpinnings of service-learning. The reader may find that these readings are a reflection of the authors' ideological positions and are not specifically about service-learning. Nonetheless these texts were formative in grounding the authors as service-learning teacher scholars. Many of these texts also provide an historical perspective within the realm of service-learning and how it has shifted and continues to shift and change as the scholarly base within the field widens.

The second section is a set of selected readings to support literacy course construction and redesign. They provide sound and concrete ways to think about making connections with partners, building the course and using various reflective tools.

The third section of resources is specific to the intersection of service-learning and teacher preparation. There is a growing body of literature where teacher educators have shared the ways in which service-learning has informed pre-service teacher development, impacted student outcomes, or served as a vehicle to sustain and support authentic and diverse nonschool-based and school-based partnerships.

The final section is a collection of resources to support faculty who seek to embrace this as a part of their scholarly agenda. These resources will provide insight as to how this type of work, intersectional by nature, bridges town and gown but also is a legitimate form of scholarship. Effective articulation of service-learning as a type of community-engaged scholarship does not have to be a secret appendage to one's research agenda but can be a salient aspect that is vibrant and innovative.

THEORETICAL AND HISTORICAL UNDERPINNINGS OF SERVICE-LEARNING

Atweh, B., Bland, D., & Ala'i, K. (2012). Education for social responsibility: Ethics and imagination in engaging teachers and students. In T. Cotton (Ed.), *Towards an education for social justice: Ethics applied to education* (pp. 13–40). Oxford: Peter Lang.

Atweh and Ala'i use a social justice framework to question how ethics are applied in education in both formal and informal ways. The authors argue for an equitable education system for all. As a case study, the authors provide evidence to suggest ways that our educational system can be the vehicle to ensure a more socially just society.

Ayers, W. (2004). *Teaching toward freedom: Moral commitment and ethical action in the classroom.* Boston: Beacon Press.

To Teach: The Journey of A Teacher (also by William Ayers) was published in 1993. Although *Teaching Toward Freedom* is not the "sequel" to the 1993 publication, this book challenges and inspires educators. Readers are called to question what it means to teach, situating the argument within the ills of society that education is expected to solve. Ayers brings a critical humanistic perspective to this work.

Billig, S., & Furco, A. (Eds.). (2002). *Service-learning through a multidisciplinary lens* (Vol. 2). Charlotte: NC: Information Age.

This edited volume provides insight into various aspects of service-learning across academic disciplines. This text is comprehensive in that it theorizes about service-learning and provides insight into how service-learning research is used and reported. The contributors to this book shed light into service-learning from diverse and global perspectives.

Bringle, R., & Hatcher, J. (1999). Reflection in service-learning: Making meaning of experience. *Educational Horizons, 77,* 179–185.

The Bringle and Hatcher article is a must-read for any novice service-learner teacher scholar. The authors offer clear definitions of service-learning through examples and non-examples. They also provide the philosophical underpinnings that frame service-learning and the reflective process by drawing on the work of John Dewey. They advocate for reflection as a salient aspect of service-learning but also offer ways in which it can be effectively and objectively assessed within a learning context.

Bringle, R., & Hatcher, J. (2002). Campus-community partnerships: The terms of engagement. *Journal of Social Issues, 58*(3), 503–516.

Within the context of higher education, Bringle and Hatcher offer insight into the interpersonal relationships at the heart of service-learning partnerships. They also offer a typology to frame the "phases of relationships" and the characteristics within each phase. This resource is valuable regardless of where one is in their development as a service-learning practitioner as a means to (re)evaluate the condition of the relationships with a community partner.

Cipolle, S. (2010). *Service-learning and social justice: Engaging students in social change.* Lanham, MD: Rowman & Littlefield.

Developing a sense of critical consciousness is what draws individuals to service-learning pedagogy. The authors outline the ways the social justice model fits within the scope service-learning. For individuals at mission-driven institutions or at institutions aligned to a religious denomination this can be helpful in identifying the ways in which service-learning pedagogy fits within the mission of the institution.

Colby, A. (2003). *Educating citizens: Preparing America's undergraduates for lives of moral and civic responsibility* (Vol. 6). Hoboken, NJ: John Wiley & Sons.

The authors of this book seek to (re)inspire faculty and rally around the call for colleges and universities to help students become more informed, thoughtful, and engaged citizens who are prepared to navigate a complex world. The questions that undergird the book are the following: What are important elements of moral and civic learning? How can higher education contribute to them effectively? What challenges do institutions face when they try to undertake efforts for moral and civic learning and how can these challenges be addressed?

Cooks, L., Scharrer, E., & Paredes, M. C. (2004). Toward a social approach to learning in community service learning. *Michigan Journal of Community Service Learning, 10*(2), 44–56.

The authors describe a social approach to learning that extends the contributions of three theoretical bodies of scholarship on learning: social constructionism, critical pedagogy, and community service-learning. The authors offer assessment concepts based on the social approach. Techniques for assessing learning are included.

Delano-Oriaran, O., Penick-Parks, M. W., & Fondrie, S. (Eds.). (2015). *The SAGE source-book of service-learning and civic engagement*. New York: SAGE.

The editors of this volume set forth to provide a comprehensive and holistic view of service-learning. There are case studies and resources to support novice and veteran service-learning teacher scholars. There are many examples and ideas that are replicable.

Hatcher, J., & Bringle, R. (1997). Reflection: Bridging the gap between service and learning. *College teaching, 45*(4), 153–158.

The focus of this article is on how to design effective reflection activities within service-learning courses. Hatcher and Bringle argue that when appropriate reflection activities are utilized, students are better able to connect the service to coursework and their learning will be enriched. The reflective activities are intended to give students a conceptual framework for learning and to support faculty so that their teaching will become more dynamic and interactive.

Landsman, J., & Lewis, C. W. (2011). *White teachers, diverse classrooms: Creating inclusive schools, building on students' diversity, and providing true educational equity*. Sterling, VA: Stylus.
Each chapter in this book offers insights into the concerns and issues students from diverse ethnic and racial groups bring to the classroom. The book encourages reflection and self-examination around high expectations for students in order to recognize unconscious biases, confront institutional racism, and adopt culturally relevant teaching practices. Unlike many other academic books, this is a great resource for a discussion group as each chapter concludes with a set of questions.

McKay, V. C., & Rozee, P. D. (2004). Characteristics of faculty who adopt community service learning pedagogy. *Michigan Journal of Community Service Learning, 10*(2), 21–33.
The authors of this research article suggest that faculty who engage in community service-learning pedagogy share many attitudes, beliefs, and values about teaching, learning, and community. The collective impact of faculty engaged in this innovative pedagogy has the potential to create a culture change within many university structures.

Stewart, T., & Webster, N. (Eds.). (2011). *Exploring cultural dynamics and tensions within service-learning*. Charlotte, NC: Information Age.
This book is about equity and social justice. The text frames the sociopolitical considerations and implications of service-learning. The perspective of this book ensures that communities are viewed from an asset-based mindset while addressing the tensions that occur as a result of personal and institutional systems of inequity. The organization of the text is thematic, based on topics, approaches, and intentions.

LOGISTICS AND COURSE CONSTRUCTION

Ballard, S., & Elmore, B. (2009). A labor of love: Constructing a service-learning syllabus. *The Journal of Effective Teaching, 9*(3), 70–76.
The focus of this article is on the construction of a syllabus that includes a service-learning component. The authors identify essential components of high-quality service-learning and offer ways to incorporate these components into appropriate courses. The process of developing a service-learning syllabus is offered in relation to course goals and objectives, service-learning activities, and reflection activities in such a

way that service-learning requirements are clearly and effectively artic-
ulated within the syllabus.

Bringle, R., & Hatcher, J. (1996). Implementing service learning in higher education. *Journal of Higher Education, 67,* 221–239.
The authors discuss service-learning as a credit-bearing educational ex-
perience, describing how students who participate in an organized service activity experience an enhanced sense of civic responsibility, differentiating between practica and service.

Cress, C. M., Collier, P. J., & Reitenauer, V. L. (2005). *Learning through serving: A student guidebook for service-learning across the disciplines.* Sterling, VA: Stylus.
The authors of this book set out to provide foundational information to
help the reader develop skills needed for student success in a service-
learning. There are examples of how to explicitly connect the service-
learning experience to the learning outcomes of a course and also included are workbook-like pages that can be infused within a course.

Heffernan, K. (2001). *Fundamentals of service-learning course construction.* Providence, RI: Brown University Campus Compact.
Heffernan's text is a comprehensive resource to support service-learn-
ing course construction. The goal of the text is to support faculty in
planning and incorporating service-learning theory and practice into
courses. Campus Compact is an organization that strives to support
faculty and institutions of higher education in developing service-learning courses and programs. The author is uniquely positioned as she has
had a long-standing relationship with Campus Compact.

Howard, J. (Ed.). (2001). *Michigan journal of community service learning: Service learning course design workbook.* University of Michigan: Office of Community Service Learning Press.
The title of this work truly lives up to its name. It is a workbook. The
author designed the text to support the planning process when developing a service-learning course. Administrative issues related to service-
learning are also addressed. The workbook is best intended for one
designing or redesigning a course to be service-learning and to use this
as part of the pre-planning before syllabus construction.

Jacoby, B., & Mutascio, P. (Eds.). (2010). *Looking in reaching out: A reflective guide for community service-learning professionals.* Providence, RI: Brown University Campus Compact.

This volume is a collection of resources, principles, best practices, and research findings about how to design, implement, and evaluate service-learning experiences. The focus of this text is to support the practitioner and ensure that desired outcomes in partnership with communities are achieved.

Kaye, C. B. (2004). *The complete guide to service learning: Proven, practical ways to engage students in civic responsibility, academic curriculum, and social action*. Minneapolis, MN: Free Spirit.

This resource is filled with activities, ideas, quotes, reflections, and resources and provides hundreds of annotated book recommendations, author interviews, and expert essays. The organization of the text makes finding resources easy. Kaye also provides examples of best practices in service-learning to help in course development.

Olivares, K. (2010). *Quick hits for service-learning*. M. A. Cooksey (Ed.). Bloomington, IN: Indiana University Press.

Quick Hits for Service-Learning presents more than eighty examples of innovative curricula, developed by educators in a wide range of disciplines, designed to combine community service with instruction and reflection. Each chapter offers tips for classroom activities for faculty to adapt to meet the desired outcomes of their course. This book serves more as reference or a resource when one is in need of ideas.

Westover, J. H. (Ed.). (2012). *Academic service-learning across disciplines: Models, outcomes, and assessment*. Champaign, IL: Common Ground.

This edited volume informs the reader of proven practices and methods for effective service-learning implementation across academic disciplines. The text provides a comprehensive introduction to service-learning, its outcomes, and approaches to effective assessment of service-learning activities by presenting a wide range of cross-disciplinary research.

SERVICE-LEARNING AND TEACHER PREPARATION

Boyle-Baise, M. (1998). Community service-learning for multicultural education: An exploratory study with preservice teachers. *Equity & Excellence in Education, 31*(2), 52–60.

This seminal article by a leading service-learning scholar provides a rationale for using service-learning in multicultural education focused on teacher preparation. Boyle-Baise explores the understandings of sixty-five pre-service teachers developed through an experience in community service-learning. Findings suggest that community service-learning for teachers should include more opportunities for reflection and a more critical concern for inequity.

Boyle-Baise, M., & Efiom, P. (2000). The construction of meaning: Learning from service learning. In C. R. O'Grady (Ed.), *Integrating service learning and multi-cultural education in colleges and universities* (pp. 209–226). Mahwah, NJ: Lawrence Erlbaum.

This oft-cited chapter is part of a collection of chapters that explores ways to integrate service-learning into multicultural education coursework, an early focus of service-learning work. It is considered by many to be a seminal piece for teacher educators.

Delano-Oriaran, O. (2014). Engaging pre-service teachers in diverse communities through service-learning: A practical guide for application. *Journal of Education for Teaching*, *40*(2), 186–188.

This article is a succinct but descriptive outline of the authentic and culturally engaging (ACE) service-learning model as a conceptual framework to guide pre-service teachers' cultural competence and cultural awareness. The author also provides a checklist practical for use in working with diverse communities.

Kinloch, V., & Smagorinsky, P. (Eds.). (2014). *Service-learning in literacy education: Possibilities for teaching and learning*. Charlotte, NC: Information Age.

This edited collection is one of the first volumes that specifically describes service-learning programs and courses designed as part of teacher education programs in the fields of literacy education, secondary English education, and elementary language arts education. The contributing authors describe the program development within the university setting. Provided is information about the rationale for their initiatives, the course designs, the outcomes of the experience, and other matters that will help literacy educators develop similar courses and experiences of their own.

Milner IV, H. R. (2010). *Start where you are, but don't stay there: Understanding diversity, opportunity gaps, and teaching in today's classrooms*. Boston: Harvard Education Press.

This book addresses the need to prepare pre-service teachers for the diverse student populations in today's classrooms. The book utilizes case studies that exemplify the challenges, pitfalls, and opportunities facing teachers in diverse classrooms. This is an easy-to-read text that offers insight into the diversity of schools and classrooms.

Nieto, S. (2005). Schools for a new majority: The role of teacher education in hard times. *The New Educator, 1* (1) , 27–43.

This article articulates the need for highly qualified teachers that are prepared for the cultural diversity and the new majority within the United States, especially in urban contexts. Neito argues for policy to rethink reforms to support student success through the utilization of best practices.

Root, S., Callahan, J., & Sepanski, J. (2002). Building teaching dispositions and service-learning practice: A multi-site study. *Michigan Journal of Community Service Learning, 8*(2), 50–60.

This research study reveals how service-learning experiences for pre-service teachers are a significant predictor of an increased commitment to teaching. Evidence from the data suggest that pre-service teachers have an increased ability to bring about social change and an increased acceptance of diversity.

Spencer, B. H., Cox-Petersen, A., & Crawford, T. (2005). Assessing the impact of service-learning on preservice teachers in an after-school program. *Teacher Education Quarterly, 32*(4), 119–135.

The study reported here uses a qualitative design to investigate the benefits of service-learning through the eyes of the pre-service teachers in an alternative learning setting, an afterschool program. Pre-service teachers participated in service-learning for approximately twenty hours and were in collaborative teaching teams. Using reflections as a primary data source, insight into pre-service teacher development and roles as pre-professionals are illuminated.

Sulentic Dowell, M-M. (2008). Academic service-learning as pedagogy: An approach to preparing pre-service teachers for urban environments. *The Journal of Teaching and Learning, 5*, 1–21.

The purpose of this article is to answer the following questions: What are the benefits to students, community, and university when academic service-learning (AS-L) is a course component? How does AS-L impact the personal intellectual growth of pre-service teachers? Using pheno-menological methodology, the results suggest that service-learning components improve and strengthen teacher education courses and pre-service teacher preparation within urban environments.

Sulentic Dowell, M-M. (2009). Transformative opportunities for community engagement within teacher education: Creating opportunities for pre-service teachers for urban environments in post-Katrina New Orleans. *Journal of Community Engagement and Higher Education, 1*(1), 1–10.

This article describes the methods of providing pre-service teachers with meaningful opportunities to engage in authentic community activities that expand their cultural horizons and frames of reference, strengthening their preparation for urban teaching. The research highlights a project that established classroom libraries in every K–8 classroom rather that delivering direct literacy instruction.

Sulentic Dowell, M-M., & Bach, J. (2012). A comparative case study of service-learning in teacher education: Rethinking benefits and challenges of partners and placements. *PRISM: A Journal of Regional Engagement*, 1 (2), 184–199.

In this piece, two literacy service-learning scholars turn their research lens inward and examine their rationales for selecting alternative partners and placements. The authors share results including benefits and challenges in an quasi-autoethnographic manner.

Sulentic Dowell, M-M., Barrera, E., Meidl, T., & Saal, L. (2015). Case studies of alternative partners and non-traditional partnerships in teacher education: Examining social justice in teacher education. In A. Tinkler, B. Tinkler, J. Strait, & V. Jagla (Eds.), *Service-learning to advance social justice in a time of radical inequality* (pp. 143–187). Charlotte, NC: Information Age.

In this chapter, four service-learning scholars from three distinct geographical locales present cases of their literacy service-learning work. Electing to work with nontraditional partners, the cases represent a local public library partner, a local public charter school, a public charter school in a different region than the pre-service teachers' college and representing an urban locale, and a case of international service-learning.

Tinkler, A., Tinkler, B., Gerstl-Pepin, C., & Mugisha, V. (2014). The promise of a community-based, participatory approach to service-learning in teacher education. *Journal of Higher Education Outreach and Engagement,18*(2), 209–232.

Using narrative inquiry, the authors highlight the opportunities and challenges within community-based research. A participatory approach to service-learning is explored and results indicate this approach can be a useful way to develop transformational service-learning relationships that support teacher education students in developing cultural competence.

Tinkler, A., Tinkler, B., Strait, J., & Jagla, V. (Eds.). (2015). *Service-learning to advance social justice in a time of radical inequality*. Charlotte, NC: Information Age.

This book returns service-leaning to its roots, social justice, presenting four sections and sixteen chapters that examine service-learning from higher education to teacher education and including unconscious bias and racial inequality and how service-learning can advance community inquiry.

Wilczenski, F. L., & Coomey, S. M. (2007). *A practical guide to service learning: Strategies for positive development in schools*. New York: Springer.

This book describes how service-learning can enable school psychologists to expand their role beyond special populations to serve students within the academic mainstream. It draws connections between the positive psychology movement, the nurturing of purpose in youth, and the benefits of service-learning. The authors provide an interesting perspective towards intervention that is parallel to reading intervention processes.

Wilhelm, J. D., Douglas, W., & Fry, S. W. (2014). *The activist learner: Inquiry, literacy, and service to make learning better*. New York: Teachers College Press.

This book explores a variety of ways teachers can integrate service-learning into the classroom. The authors demonstrate how inquiry-based teaching with service-learning outcomes cultivates and rewards literacy. Through the pursuit of service-learning projects, students develop and apply literacy and disciplinary knowledge, experience real-world implications, and learn to think in more connected ways.

Villegas, A., & Lucas, T. (2002). *Educating culturally responsive teachers: A coherent approach*. Albany: State University of New York.

This book presents an approach to educating culturally responsive teachers. The authors focus on the importance of recruiting and preparing a diverse teaching force. The authors reconceptualize multicultural education by providing a curriculum proposal for culturally responsive teaching and guidelines for institutional support structures.

PUBLICLY-ENGAGED SCHOLARSHIP AND COMMUNITY-ENGAGED SCHOLARSHIP

Abes, E., Jackson, G., & Jones, S. R. (2002). Factors that motivate and deter faculty use of service-learning. *Michigan Journal of Community Service Learning*, 9(1) 5–17.

The purpose of this research was to determine the factors that motivate and deter faculty use of service-learning. The authors identify factors such as logistical support, evidence of increasing course outcomes, and instruction in how to implement service-learning that either motivated or deterred faculty from engaging in service-learning pedagogy. This resource is helpful in reflecting on the type of support to seek out in order to ensure the effectiveness of a service-learning course.

Doberneck, D. M., Glass, C. R., & Schweitzer, J. (2010). From rhetoric to reality: A typology of publicly engaged scholarship. *Journal of Higher Education Outreach and Engagement,* *14*(4), 5–35.

Using a faculty perspective, authors have created a typology of publicly engaged scholarship based upon faculty descriptions of their scholarly work. The data represents various types of institutions including public and private institutions. A fourteen-category typology that emerged from the data and literature comprises four types of publicly engaged research and creative activities, five types of publicly engaged instruction, four types of publicly engaged service, and one type of publicly engaged commercialized activity. The findings are a useful tool in supporting faculty development programs and career decision-making scholars on the tenure track.

Furco, A., & Billig, S. (Eds.). (2002). *Service-learning: The essence of the pedagogy* (Vol. 1). Charlotte, NC: Information Age.

This edited volume is intended to display service-learning as a multifaceted pedagogy. The text offers a broad range of topics including defining service-learning, theorizing service-learning, and analyzing methodologies within the study of service-learning. Unlike other texts, the book frames both qualitative and quantitative methodologies to demonstrate the ways in which the impact of service-learning is measured.

WORKS CITED

Achieve Brown County. (2015). Retrieved from http://www.achievebrowncounty.org/

Allam, C., & Zerkin, B. (1993). The case for integrating service-learning into teacher preparation programs. *Generator, 13*, 11–13.

Allington, R. (2001). *What really matters for struggling readers: Designing research-based programs* (3rd ed.). New York: Addison-Wesley.

Allington, R. (2002a). *Big brother and the national reading curriculum: How ideology trumped evidence.* Portsmouth, NH: Heinemann.

Allington, R. (2002b). What I've learned about effective reading instruction from a decade of studying exemplary elementary classroom teachers. *Phi Delta Kappan, 83*, 740–747.

Allington, R. (2004, March). Setting the record straight. *Educational Leadership, 61*(6), 22–25.

Allington, R. (2006). Critical factors in designing an effective reading intervention for struggling readers. In C. Cummins (Ed.), *Understanding and implementing reading first initiatives* (pp. 127–138). Newark, DE: International Reading Association.

Altwerger, B. (2005). *Reading for profit: How the bottom line leaves kids behind.* Portsmouth, NH: Heinemann.

American Educational Research Association. (1991). In M. Cochran-Smith and K. Zeichner (Eds.), *Studying teacher education: The report of the AERA panel on research and teacher education.* Mahwah, NJ: Lawrence Erlbaum.

American Federation of Teachers. (2012). *Raising the bar: Aligning and elevating teacher preparation and the teaching profession.* Washington, DC: Author.

Appelt Slick, G. (Ed.). (1995). *Preparing new teachers: Operating successful field experience programs.* Thousand Oaks, CA: Corwin Press.

Au, W. (2005-06). Conversations on quality: An interview with Gloria Ladsen-Billings. *Rethinking Schools, 20*, 36–37.

Ayers, W., & Ford, P. (1996). *City kids, city teachers.* New York: The New Press.

Barnes, C. (2006). Preparing preservice teachers to teach in a culturally responsive way. *The Negro Educational Review, 57*(1–2), 85–100.

Billig, S., & Furco, A. (Eds.). (2002). *Service-learning through a multidisciplinary lens* (Vol. 2). Charlotte: NC: Information Age.

Boyle-Baise, M. (1998). Community service-learning for multicultural education: An exploratory study with preservice teachers. *Equity & Excellence in Education, 31*(2), 52–60.

Boyle-Baise, M. (2002). *Multicultural service learning: Educating teachers in diverse communities.* New York: Teachers College Press.

Boyle-Baise, M., & Kilbane, J. (2000). What really happens? A look inside service-learning for multicultural teacher education. *Michigan Journal of Community Service Learning, 7*(1), 54–64.

Boyle-Baise, M., & Sleeter, C. (2000). Community-based service learning for multicultural teacher education. *Educational Foundations, 14*(2), 33–50.

Bringle, R. G. & Hatcher, J. A. (1996). Implementing service learning in higher education. *Journal of High Education, 67,* 221-239.

Butin, D. (2003). Of what use is it? Multiple conceptions of service learning within education. *Teachers College Record, 105*(9), 1674–1692.

Campus Compact. (2015). Retrieved from http://compact.org/

Canning, C. (1991). What teachers say about reflection. *Educational Leadership, 48*(6), 18–21.

Carnegie Foundation for the Advancement of Teaching. (2015). Retrieved from http://www.carnegiefoundation.org/

Coan, P. M. (1977). *Ellis Island interviews: In their own words.* New York: Facts on File.

Cochran-Smith, M. (2000). Blind vision: Unlearning racism in teacher education. *Harvard Educational Review, 70,* 157–185.

Coffman, A., & Patterson, R. (2014). *Teacher residencies: Redefining preparation through partnerships.* Washington, DC: National Education Association.

Coles, G. (2003). *Reading the naked truth: Literacy, Legislation, and Lies.* Portsmouth, NH: Heinemann.

Compton-Lilly, C. (2004). *Confronting racism, poverty, and power: Classroom strategies to change the world.* Portsmouth, NH: Heinemann.

Conrad, D., & Hedin, D. (1991). School-based community service: What we know from research and theory. *Phi Delta Kappan, 72*(10), 743–749.

Darling-Hammond, L. (2006a). Constructing 21st-century teacher education. *Journal of Teacher Education , 57*(3), 300–314.

Darling-Hammond, L. (2006b). *Powerful teacher education: Lessons from exemplary programs.* San Francisco: Jossey-Bass.

Darling-Hammond, L. (2010a). Teacher education and the American future. *Journal of Teacher Education, 61*(1–2), 35–47.

Darling-Hammond, L. (2010b). *The flat world and education: How America's commitment to equity will determine our future.* New York: Teachers College Press.

Darling-Hammond, L. (2014a). One piece of the whole. *American Educator, 38*(1), 4–13, 44.

Darling-Hammond, L. (2014b). Forward. In H. R. Milner & K. Lomotey (Eds.), *Handbook of Urban Education* (pp. xi–xiii). New York: Routledge.

Darling-Hammond, L., Holtzman, D., Gatlin, S., & Heilig, J. (2005). Does teacher preparation matter? Evidence about teacher certification, Teach for America, and teacher effectiveness. *Education Policy Analysis Archives, 13*(42).

Davis, J., & Bauman, K. (2013, September). *School enrollment in the United States: Population characteristics.* Washington, DC: United States Census Bureau.

Delano-Oriaran, O. (2012). Infusing Umoja, an authentic and culturally engaging service-learning model, into multicultural education. *International Journal of Teaching and Learning in Higher Education, 24*(3), 403–414.

Delpit, L. (1995). *Other people's children.* New York: New Press.

Dewey, J. (1922). *Democracy and education.* New York: Macmillan.

Dewey, J. (1938). *Experience and education.* New York: Collier.

Diller, J. V., & Moule, J. (2005). *Cultural competence: A primer for educators.* Thomson/Wadsworth.

Discovery Channel. (1993). *The promised land.* Bethesda, MD: Nicholas Lemann.

Domonoske, C. (2014). Word watch: Segregated from its history, how "'ghetto" lost its meaning. *NPR: Code Switch: Race and Identity, Remixed.* Retrieved from http://www.npr.org/sections/codeswitch/2014/04/27/306829915/segregated-from-its-history-how-ghetto-lost-its-meaning

Dweck, C. (2006). *Mindset: The new psychology of success.* New York: Random House.

Eyler, J., Giles, D., & Schmiede, A. (1996). *A practioner's guide to reflection in service-learning: Student voices and reflections.* Nashville: Vanderbilt University Press.

Feistritzer, E. (2011). *Profile of teachers in the U.S.* Washington, DC: National Center for Education Information.

Finn, P. (1998). *Literacy with an attitude.* Albany, NY: State University Press.

Flannery, D., & Ward, K. (1999). Service learning: A vehicle for developing cultural competence in health education. *American Journal of Health Behavior, 23,* 323–331.

Freedman, S., Simons, E., Kalnin, J., & Casareno, A. (1999). *Inside city schools.* New York: Teachers College Press.

Furco, A. (1996). Service-learning: A balanced approach to experiential education. In B. Taylor (Ed.), *Expanding boundaries: Service and learning* (pp. 2–6).

Furco, A. (2000, October). *Service learning in teacher education: A review of the research.* Paper presented at the Connections: Infusing service-learning into teacher preparation meeting sponsored by the California State University Office of Community Service Learning, Los Angeles, CA.

Garan, E. (2002). *Resisting reading mandates.* Portsmouth, NH: Heinemann.

Garan, E. (2004). *In defense of our children.* Portsmouth, NH: Heinemann.

Gay, G. (2000). *Culturally responsive teaching: Theory, research, and practice.* New York: Teachers College Press.

Gay, G. (2002). Preparing for culturally responsive teaching. *Journal of Teacher Education. 53*(2), 106–116.

Gay, G. (2010). *Culturally responsive teaching: Theory, research, and practice* (2nd ed.). New York: Teachers College Press.

González, N., Moll, L., & Amanti, C. (2005). *Funds of knowledge: Theorizing practices in households, communities, and classrooms.* Mahwah, NJ: Lawrence Erlbaum.

Hatcher, J., & Bringle, R. (1997). Reflection: Bridging the gap between service and learning. *College teaching, 45*(4), 153–158.

Howard, T. C. (2003). Culturally relevant pedagogy: Ingredients for critical teacher reflection. *Theory Into Practice, 42*(3), 195–202.

Howard, T. C., & Milner, H. R. (2014). Teacher preparation for urban schools. In H. R. Milner & K. Lomotey (Eds.), *Handbook of urban education* (pp. 199–216). New York: Routledge.

International Reading Association. (2003, May). *Policy update addressing urban needs.* Paper presented at a meeting of the City Heights Project of San Diego, CA.

Irvine, J. J. (2003). *Educating teachers for diversity: Seeing with a cultural eye.* New York: Teachers College Press.

Jaquith, C. (1995). Organizing and managing field experience programs. In G. Appelt Slick, (Ed.), *Preparing new teachers: Operating successful field experience programs.* Thousand Oaks, CA: Corwin Press.

Koppich, J. E., & Merseth, K. K. (2000). *Studies of excellence in teacher education: Preparation in a five-year program.* Washington, DC: American Association of Colleges for Teacher Education.

Kozol, J. (2006). *The shame of the nation: The restoration of apartheid schooling in America.* New York: Crown Publishing.

Ladson-Billings, G. (1994). *The dreamkeepers.* San Francisco: Jossey-Bass.

Ladson-Billings, G. (1995). Toward a theory of culturally relevant pedagogy. *American Educational Research Journal, 32*(3), 465–491.

Ladson-Billings, G. (2000). Reading between the lines and beyond the pages: A culturally relevant approach to literacy teaching. In M. A. Gallego & S. Hollingsworth (Eds.), *What counts as literacy: Challenging the school standard* (pp. 139–152). New York: Teachers College Press.

Larkin, J. M., & Sleeter, C. (1995). *Developing multicultural teacher education curricula.* Albany: State University of New York Press.

Madison, C. A.. & Riis, J. (1971). *How the other half lives.* (Unabridged replication of a 1901 edition.). New York: Dover.

Mason, P. A., & Schumm, J. (Eds.). (2003). *Promising practices for urban reading instruction*. Newark, DE: International Reading Association.

Maxwell, L. (2014, August 21). U.S. school enrollment hits majority-minority milestone. *Education Week*. Retrieved from http://www.edweek.org/ew/projects/ changing-demographics.html?cmp=ENL-EU-NEWS

Meidl, T., & Nissen, J. (2015). Dismantling the perceived hierarchy: A shared intellectual endeavor between faculty and student affairs. In Delano-Oriaran, O., Penick-Parks, M. W., & Fondrie, S. (Eds.), *The SAGE sourcebook of service-learning and civic engagement*. SAGE.

Merriam-Webster. (2015). Retrieved from http://www.merriam-webster.com/dictionary/ ghetto

Meyer, R. (2010). *Official portraits and unofficial counterportraits of "at-risk" students*. New York: Routledge/Taylor & Francis.

Milner, H. R., & Lomotey, K. (2014). *Handbook of urban education*. New York: Routledge.

Myers, C., & Pickeral, T. (1997). Service-learning: An essential process for preparing teachers as transformational leaders in the reform of public education. In J. Erickson and J. Anderson (Eds.), *Learning with the community: Concepts and models for service-learning in teacher education* (pp. 13–41). Sterling, VA: Stylus Publishing.

National Center for Educational Statistics. (2014). *The Condition of Education*. Washington, DC: Author.

Potter, J. The challenge of education for active citizenship. *Education + Training, 44*(2), 57-66.

Root, S. C. (1994). Service learning in teacher education: A third rationale. *Michigan Journal of Community Service Learning, 1*(1), 94–97.

Root, S. C. (1997). School-based service: A review of research for teacher educators. In J. Erickson & J. Anderson (Eds.), *Learning with the community: Concepts and models for service-learning in teacher education* (pp. 42–72). Washington, DC: American Association for Higher Education.

Shannon, P. (2001). *Becoming political, too*. Portsmouth, NH: Heinemann.

Shannon, P. (2007). *Reading against democracy: The broken promises of reading instruction*. Portsmouth, NH: Heinemann.

Sulentic Dowell, M-M. (2008). Academic service learning as pedagogy: An approach to preparing pre-service teachers for urban environments. *The Journal of Teaching and Learning, 5*(2), 1–21.

Sulentic Dowell, M-M. (2009). Transformative opportunities for community engagement within teacher education: Creating opportunities for pre-service teachers for urban environments in post-Katrina New Orleans. *Journal of Community Engagement and Higher Education, 1*(1), 1–10.

Sulentic Dowell, M-M., & Bach, J. (2012). A comparative case study of service-learning in teacher education: Rethinking benefits and challenges of partners and placements. *PRISM: A Journal of Regional Engagement, 1* (2), 184–199.

Sulentic Dowell, M-M., Barrera, E., Meidl, T. & Saal, L. (2015). Case studies of alternative partners and non-traditional partnerships in teacher education: Examining social justice in teacher education. In A. Tinkler, B. Tinkler, J. Strait, & V. Jagla, (Eds.), *Service-learning to advance social justice in a time of radical inequality* (pp. 143–187). Charlotte, NC: Information Age Publishers.

Tai-Seale, T. (2001). Liberating service learning and applying new practice. *College Teaching, 49*(1), 14–18.

Tharp, R. (2014, September). Residency: Can it transform teaching the way it did medicine? *Phi Delta Kappan, 96*, 1–8.

United States Census Bureau. (2011). Retrieved from http://www.census.gov/

University of Mississippi. (1994). *Goin' to Chicago* [videorecording]. Jackson, MS: George King and Associates.

Villegas, A., & Lucas, T. (2002). *Educating culturally responsive teachers: A coherent approach*. Albany: State University of New York Press.

Zlotkowski, E. (2007). Pedagogy and engagement. In Campus Compact (Ed.), *Introduction to service-learning toolkit: Readings and resources for faculty* (pp. 63–80). Boston: Campus Compact, Brown. (Original work published in 1999).

ABOUT THE AUTHORS

Margaret-Mary Sulentic Dowell, PhD, is professor of literacy and urban education at Louisiana State University, Baton Rouge, where she also serves as director of the LSU Writing Project and coordinator of the Elementary Grades 1–5 Teacher Education Program. Sulentic Dowell's research agenda is focused on literacy in urban settings, specifically the complexities of literacy leadership; providing access to literature, writing, and the arts; and service-learning as a pathway to preparing pre-service teachers to teach literacy authentically in urban environs. She was editor of the *Literacy and Social Responsibility* ejournal from 2009–2014. Sulentic Dowell spent fifteen years as an educator in the Waterloo Iowa Community Schools and was a service-learning faculty fellow at the University of Southern Mississippi, Hattiesburg. She is also former assistant superintendent for sixty-four elementary schools in the East Baton Rouge Parish School System.

Tynisha D. Meidl, PhD, is associate professor of teacher education at St. Norbert College in De Pere, Wisconsin, where she also serves as the co-chair of the teacher education program. She earned her PhD in curriculum and instruction from Pennsylvania State University. Meidl teaches literacy courses aimed at assisting pre-service teachers and preparing them to enter the classroom as proficient literacy teachers. Her research expertise includes curriculum planning for linguistically and culturally diverse student populations and service-learning as pedagogy, as well as Freirean-based approaches in literacy classrooms. Prior to joining the faculty at St. Norbert, she taught in the Baltimore City

Public Schools and in the Rio Grande Valley in Texas. Meidl is a Teach for America alumna and current co-editor of the *Literacy and Social Responsibility* ejournal.

www.ingramcontent.com/pod-product-compliance
Lightning Source LLC
Chambersburg PA
CBHW020357270326
41926CB00007B/477